Zana and the Bumbling Genie

Padmini Sankar

Om Books International

First published in 2025

Om Books International

Corporate & Editorial Office
A-12, Sector 64, Noida 201 301
Uttar Pradesh, India
Phone: +91 120 477 4100
Email: editorial@ombooks.com
Website: www.ombooksinternational.com

Sales Office
107, Ansari Road, Darya Ganj,
New Delhi 110 002, India
Phone: +91 11 4000 9000
Email: sales@ombooks.com
Website: www.ombooks.com

ISBN: 978-93-6395-736-7

Printed in India

10 9 8 7 6 5 4 3 2 1

To Misha and Ruhi

And to all those, children or adults, who believe in magic and miracles, this is for you.

Acknowledgements

I've always wanted to write a children's fantasy with an Indian character at its centre. *Zara and the Bumbling Genie* is the culmination of my dreams and desires as well as my childhood reading. For this I owe thanks to many.

First of all, special thanks to the publisher, Mr Ajay Mago who saw potential in the book.

My approachable editor Dr Kirti Pathak for her sharp inputs and suggestions.

Palak Kumra whose sketches brought the book to life.

I'd next like to thank my literary agent Suhail Mathur of the Book Bakers Literary Agency for believing in my book and taking it on.

Very special thanks to my wonderful writing group—Heidi, Linda, Mubeena and Avril. I can honestly say that this book would not be the same without all your encouragement and constructive feedback. I owe you big.

I'd like to thank Rachel Hamilton for her guidance, and my young beta readers Akshara, Anoushka and Anya for their useful comments. To Darlene Tezdiker, thank you for all the time and effort in taking my author photos; to the Gundans, the Ganapathy family and my book club for their unstinting support; to Chandana, Latha, Kala, Viji and Gay, for showing the way.

To my family – my husband, Shankar, thank you for just being you, and to my children Kartik, Preeti and Komal, for your reality checks. And finally, thank you to my readers who must have picked up this book because they believe in magic.

Contents

Chapter 1

A Surprise Visitor

It should have been strange for Zara to be talking to a genie in the middle of the night, but here she was. Zara squinted, trying to make out the details of the thing that stood in front of her. It was a huge man with a funny-looking tuft of hair on his bald head and tiny gold hoops in his ears. He wore a striped vest, something like a prison uniform. For a moment, she lost her voice. Then she opened her mouth wide to let out an ear-piercing scream, but remembered just in time that Mom and Dad would wake up and scold her for being out in the balcony so late at night, so she gave just a tiny, frightened squeak.

"Don't be scared, sweet little girl," said the strange-looking man-monster. "I won't hurt you. I'm the genie who lives in this tamarind tree."

He pointed to the big, leafy tree whose branches fell into their first-floor apartment. Long brown pods, like giant beans, hung from its branches. The monster spoke in a soft, hoarse voice as if he had a very sore throat. Zara squinted harder. He was a lot like the genie in Aladdin, except for the striped vest.

"Oops!" The genie's hand swooped out and caught a baby bird mid-way as it was falling out of its nest. "There you go," he said in his sore-throat voice, gently putting the tiny creature back into its home. Then, turning once again to Zara, he said, "These li'l 'uns keep falling out in their sleep. They don't even know they've fallen out and I've caught 'em. They're still sleeping."

A genie who rescued baby birds couldn't be that bad. Zara found her voice. "You can't be a real genie," she said. "Genies don't live in trees. They live in urns and lamps and wait to be summoned.

And they live in Arabia, not here in India. So don't think you can fool me." Then another thought struck her. "Oh, if you're a robber, I'm very sorry, but we're not rich."

"I *am* a real genie," he said, "but a genie who can't do no real magic. My name's Joom. And yours?"

"You haven't answered me," said Zara, ignoring his question. "How come you live here in this old tamarind tree and not in an urn or lamp?"

The genie turned and looked around. His voice became almost a whisper. "That's a long story. I'll tell you another time." He looked around again, as if assuring himself that all was okay, and continued in a louder voice, "But tell me, why are you so sad? And why are you out so late at night?"

Zara thought for a moment. The genie seemed so kind. And it would be nice to tell *someone* her problem.

"Fifty lakhs," she said. "That's why I'm sad. We need fifty lakhs for my operation, and I don't know how my Mom and Dad will ever get that much of money."

The genie's face scrunched up. "Goodness. That's a lot of money."

"Yes, mine is also a long story, like yours. Or maybe not so long. It's actually quite a short story."

"Well, why don't you tell me the *whole* story? Perhaps I can help."

The genie plonked himself on the floor of the balcony. Zara sat opposite him.

"Start with your name, little girl," he said. "I've told you mine. It's Joom."

"My name's Zara, and I'm eleven years old. Until a year ago, I could see very well. But then, something went wrong with my eyes." Zara paused, thinking of that awful day when her entire world became hazy. "I can see properly only when I squint very hard."

"Oh dear. That must be so difficult for you."

"Yes, I can only see clearly when I wear horrible, thick glasses. I hate them. Otherwise, everything is blurry. I can just about make out colours and shapes. If I squint, I see clearly, but I can't keep my eyes squeezed up all the time, can I?"

The genie nodded. "Who can keep their eyes squeezed up all the time? No one."

"But a special doctor saw me today and said I'd become totally blind in three months unless I have an operation. He didn't tell me directly, but I overheard him saying so to my Mom and Dad."

"Well, that's a good thing, isn't it? There's a solution. The operation."

"I wish it were so simple," said Zara, "but you see, genie, the surgery can be done only in Los Angeles. And that is so far from New Delhi."

"What is this Boss Danglies?"

Zara giggled. "Not Boss Danglies. Los Angeles," she said, drawing out each word. "It's very far away. My Mom and Dad don't even have enough money for the plane tickets, let alone fifty lakhs. That's how much this surgery would cost."

"Oh," said the genie, scratching his head. "Don't worry. There is always a way. I'm over two thousand years old and know a thing or two."

"Over two thousand years old! You must have millions of wrinkles."

"I do," said the genie, pushing his face forward. "Can you see?"

Zara couldn't see him very well in the dark although she squinted, but when she put her hand up to push back her hair, she accidentally touched his face.

"Oh my goodness! It's like cheesecloth," she said. "You must have a million wrinkles. Imagine, you've been living in this tamarind tree all this while and I never knew. Will you be my friend?"

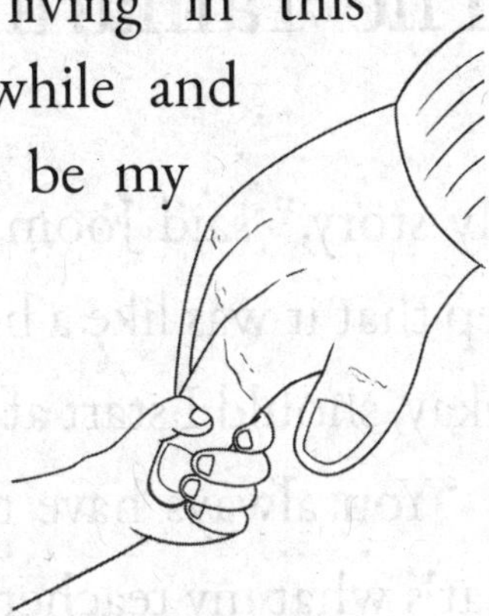

"Of course," said the genie. He put out his finger, and Zara shook it. His entire hand was too big for her to shake. "And please call me Joom."

"It's a deal," said Zara. "Now, Joom, tell me your story and how you've come to live in this tree."

"Certainly," said Joom, and stretched himself out a little more.

◆◆◆

Chapter 2

The Tamarind Tree Home

"My story," said Joom, and sighed so long and deep that it was like a hot breeze hitting her face. "Okay, should I start at the beginning?"

"You always have to start at the beginning. That's what my teachers say."

"Alright then." And here, Joom stretched out a wee bit more. "Little girl, I'm not a very good genie. I make lots of mistakes and bungle things up.

"It was okay for me because my first master was very kind and gave me many chances. His name was Abu Moosa, and he lived over two thousand years ago. But then, a terrible earthquake took place, everything was destroyed, and an evil man became my master. I can't tell you how cruel he was. He'd sometimes whip me out of boredom. But that was not as bad as some of the things he made me do. I bungled up those too, and he said I did it on purpose."

Zara leaned forward. "Oh no, Joom. I can't imagine how hard it must have been for you to be whipped for no reason. But what were some of the bad things he made you do?"

Joom was silent for a few moments. "I don't think you should know. You're just eleven years old."

"But can you tell me why you ran away?"

Joom looked around and continued, "The last spell he made me do was the worst, most evil spell of all. And I bungled that up too. So, the evil master said he'd lock me up in a heavy urn and throw me into the bottom of the deepest ocean, where I'd never be found." He paused, scratching his head, and his voice went down to a very low whisper. "I don't even want to talk about that last spell, little Zara. That's when I made up my mind to run away. And I ran as far as I could.

"I was a strong young genie then and knew some magic so, I could run and fly and even swim underwater. I decided to put as much distance as possible between us, and that's why I came to India all the way from the golden sands of Arabia."

Zara could feel his body tremble. "I've escaped the Evil One's clutches, but I don't know for how long. He's after me." His voice was shaking, and Zara could see him looking around as if to make sure no one was around.

"It's good you ran away, Joom" said Zara, patting his arm. "That was the right thing to do, rather than casting evil spells on others. They say cowards run away, but you were brave to run away. By the way, what's the name of your evil master?"

Joom trembled. "H-his name? If I say his name out aloud, I'm afraid that he'll come. It's like summoning an evil spirit."

"Of course not, genie," said Zara. "You're safe in this tamarind tree. And I'm here, right next to you. And my father and mother know how to deal with bad people. My Dad is really clever. So, nothing will happen if you tell me."

The genie gasped. Zara could hear him swallow, hear the frightened gulp. "Gorgonzola," he said. "He calls himself Mr Gorgonzola."

The genie suddenly went still and quiet, and looked around. His body once again started trembling.

"There, there, Joom. Nobody's come. I'm here beside you. Don't feel scared," said Zara, patting his arm. "Besides, Gorgonzola is the name of a cheese. It's supposed to be smelly and some people say it tastes like vomit. Is your Mr

Gorgonzola smelly?" Zara smiled when she asked this.

"Shhh!" Joom said in alarm. "He may hear you." He once again looked over his shoulder, as if to make sure. Then he whispered to Zara, "He does sometimes smell bad, but I think that's his bad nature and evil mind. But he uses a lot of strong perfume to cover his smell."

Zara gave him another pat. "Don't be afraid, genie. As long as I'm here, he won't be able to get you. And if I ever get to meet him, I'll hold my nose."

Joom smiled. "Thank you, little Zara."

"Besides, you have such a nice home in this tree. Don't worry, you're safe."

"Is that so? I really like living here."

"I like this tree too," said Zara. "It makes the balcony look like a green room. I know, let's make a pact."

"What's a pact?" Joom asked. "Is it like the heavy load I had to carry?"

"That's a pack, not a pact," explained Zara. "A pact is like a deal. We'll meet here every night, or as often as we can, and tell each other our stories. And we'll both think a way out of our problems."

"Jiggery jaggery," said Joom, singing happily. "Let's shake hands."

Zara couldn't shake all of his hand, but he put out two fingers. She clasped them with her small hands and shook them up and down.

"Jiggery jaggery," sang back Zara. "I don't know what that means, but I like those words. See you tomorrow night, Joom."

◆◆◆

Chapter 3

Darkness Everywhere

"Zara! Wake up! You'll be late for school."

Zara rubbed her eyes, turned the other side and slid deeper under the blanket.

"No, Mom, it can't already be six-thirty," she murmured sleepily.

"It's six forty-five."

Six forty-five! Zara sat up straight. She'd overslept by fifteen minutes. But what a nice dream she'd been dreaming, chatting and laughing with a genie.

"Here you are," said Mom, putting Zara's thick, heavy glasses on her pert little nose.

Immediately, the room came into focus—her study table in one corner, her books arranged neatly on the bookshelf, and Mom, already dressed and ready in a crisp cotton salwar-kameez.

"Mom, you know I can put on my glasses myself," said Zara. "They're lying right next to me. I'm not a baby."

"Okay, tomorrow I'll let you put them on, I promise," said Mom. "Hurry up and get ready."

"Yes, Mom, I can manage. *Myself.*" Zara stressed the last word. She hated all this fussing, people helping her, being extra nice to her just because she couldn't see well. She didn't want any special treatment. She hated taking any help from anybody, including Mom. And she hated wearing these ugly glasses too, but couldn't do without them.

It was not that Zara was *born* with poor eyesight. She began brushing her teeth, recalling the day, almost a year ago, when her world came tumbling down. It was a Saturday, and she had woken up with a pounding headache. It was as if someone was hammering her head from inside. Then she saw stars. She got out of bed and called out for Mom. She felt herself falling. She heard a scream and then total blackness engulfed her.

Even now, Zara wasn't sure what exactly happened, because when she woke up, she was in a hospital bed with a bandage over her eyes. Someone with a nice voice—she remembered that the voice was very kind—spoke to her, patting her on the shoulder. "Awake now? Don't you worry, your Mom and Dad are next door. I'll get them."

She felt bewildered. *Why can't I see?* Then, a horrible thought came to her mind. "Am I blind?" she asked.

The voice went, "Tsk! Tsk! Of course not. We'll be removing your bandages today. Let Dr Ravi come, and they'll be off."

She heard her door open and knew it was Mom and Dad from the rushed footsteps. They both hugged her. She could smell Mom's familiar perfume, a sandal-wood-soap fragrance, and Dad smelt of his usual coffee and carbolic soap.

"Mom, Dad, what's happened to me? Why can't I see?"

"You will be able to see, but you need glasses," said Mom gently. "The doctor will explain."

"It was lucky that we got you to the hospital just in time," said Dad.

And when the kind doctor did remove her bandages, she found she could see, but everything was so fuzzy. It was as if the world was a smudged painting.

"Everything looks blurred," she said.

The doctor patted her on her back. "You've been a very brave little girl. We need to get you special glasses so that you can see clearly."

And that was the beginning of her new life, where she had to wear these thick glasses with an ugly black frame. Only then could she see clearly.

Without those glasses, she could make out things only if she screwed up her eyes tight. The doctor used some words to describe her condition, some *macular* something, and the grown-ups all looked very serious. But at least she could read books and watch TV, although she wasn't allowed to do some of the very vigorous PE activities like playing basketball or long jump.

Only now, since her check-up yesterday morning, things seemed even grimmer! Dr Ravi said she'd become blind unless she had that special operation. Three months. That was it.

Zara continued brushing. *Scrub, scrub, scrub*, first the upper, then the lower teeth, using a circular motion. Oh dear! What a strange meeting she'd had last night. Was it real or had she dreamt it all? She'd gone to bed at one in the morning after the genie—Joom, wasn't that his name?—promised that they'd meet the next night.

"Zara, are you done? I've made you your favourite breakfast—pancakes with maple syrup."

"Yes, Mom, almost done," shouted back

Zara. "Five minutes please." She straightened her bedsheet and pillow and folded her quilt. She took a last look at herself in the mirror to make sure she was neat and clean. Just as she was about to open her bedroom door, she heard her parents talking in lowered voices.

"Selling the ancestral house is the best thing to do. It'll go for a huge sum."

"Are you serious, Sameer? You really want to sell it? It's been in your family for over a hundred years." Her mother's voice sounded sad and shocked.

Zara's ears pricked up. Ever since her eyesight had become worse, her ears seemed to have become sharper. Was Dad selling their beautiful ancestral house in Chandni Chowk, the mansion that was in ruins but which he stubbornly held on to? It was a hundred years old and had beautiful flooring and huge rooms with high ceilings. Dad's grandfather had bought this house and he had inherited it. Of course, nobody could live in it,

but Dad had said once he retired, he'd sell it and buy a modern house with the money. Mom had said he'd never do it, and if he wanted to sell it, he had to do it now, but Dad had always argued that the land value would increase and he'd get much more for it many years later. It was his golden egg.

"Mom! Dad! You are not selling dear great-grandpa's house."

Her parents looked up.

"Good morning, Zara," said Dad.

Zara did not return her father's greeting. "Dad, you can't sell great-grandpa's house. I heard you."

Her parents looked at each other. "Sit down, child, and have your breakfast," said Dad.

"No. Dad, don't change the topic. I heard you. I know this surgery is expensive, but we can find another way to get the money." Zara's cheeks were flushed, and a little voice inside her said, *what other way?*

"We don't want you to worry about money matters. That's for us parents to worry over, not for you. And I promise you, somehow we'll get it." Dad looked at her with a stern expression.

"But Dad—"

"Enough! Always arguing, aren't you? As feisty as ever," said Mom. Zara scowled. That was her nickname at home, and even at school. Feisty Zara. Always ready to argue her point.

Then, on a kinder note, Dad said, "Look, you just work hard, and we'll take care of the other stuff. Is that clear?"

Zara nodded. Both Mom and Dad had their 'strict teacher' looks on. They meant business. A NO was a NO.

And that was the end of the topic.

Zara was very proud of her father. Dr Sameer Kumar, popularly known as Dr Sameer, was the only teacher in her school with a PhD. She was proud of her mom, Seema Kumar, too, but more so of Dad. He was the Head of Math in her school, Summerdale High, while Mom taught social studies to the grade 6 students. Summerdale High was the best, and the most expensive school in the city. Since her father was the Head of Math in the school, Zara's tuition was free.

Your dad is the best," some of the senior school kids told her. "He explains things so well."

And another time, one of her friend's sisters went up to Zara during recess and said, "You're Dr Sameer's daughter, aren't you? If it weren't for your dad, I would have hated math. It's now my favourite subject."

Not that Zara strutted around school like a proud peacock because her Dad was so respected. She was just like the other kids, getting into the usual mischief. And, thank goodness, she wasn't in the class Mom taught, but in a different section. How strange it would be to be taught by your own mother!

Mom had warned her about not arguing, especially with her teachers. "I don't want any complaints about you," she said.

Zara had promised she'd never argue, but she still joined in the class pranks. Like that last time, when they'd hidden the whiteboard markers so that poor Mrs Abraham, the history teacher, had to send one of them to the office to fetch more markers, and they'd had a mini break. Or when they tossed that paper ball around the class, making sure the teacher didn't see it, throwing it whenever her back was turned to them. Oh, what fun it was! Of course, now, Zara couldn't play some of these games because of her poor eyesight, but with the help of her friends, she still participated in the pranks.

But things had changed ever since Mr Boyle became headmaster. Dad no longer occupied an important place. Zara saw that both Dad and Mom were not very happy. The earlier headmaster, Mr Dimpleby, used to consider Dad his 'right-hand man'. Dad practically ran the school along with Mr Dimpleby.

That morning when she'd got up late, Dad parked his small, second-hand car in its usual place, a spot reserved for him as Head of Math.

"Hurry up or we'll be disciplined," said Mom.

"Hahaha." Dad laughed without mirth. "So, we are being treated like school kids."

Zara had overheard her parents talking about the new school rules many times ever since Mr Boyle had taken over. Arriving late seven times meant a day's pay was cut. They had a special card which they had to insert into a machine. "It's so demeaning. It's like we're construction workers," Dad had said when the rule was introduced.

The teachers came half an hour before school started. Sometimes, they had meetings during this first half-hour. Zara was quite happy coming a little earlier. Her friends, Pixie and Mimi, were usually early too, so they had a bit of fun together.

She skipped along beside her parents into the reception where they had to clock in. And then she froze. So did her mother and father. A black figure was standing by the table where the machine was kept. It was Mr Boyle.

◆◆◆

Chapter 4

The New Headmaster

Mr Boyle, the headmaster, was a large man with a small moustache. He was always impeccably dressed in expensive suits, and today too, he was wearing a black suit with a red tie and a white starched shirt visible from beneath.

Zara noticed both her parents stiffen when they saw him. But she was a well-mannered girl, so she greeted him politely.

"Good morning, sir."

"Ho, ho, ho! Good morning to the Kumar family," said Mr Boyle, showing all his sharp teeth. The corners of his little black moustache touched his nose when he smiled. “Good to see you here fresh and early for a change.”

Zara saw Mom and Dad change colour. Mom gave a stiff smile, Dad nodded. They inserted their cards into the timer-machine and walked out without a word.

“What does he think of himself, saying we’re early for a change,” said Dad as soon as they were out of earshot.

“Oh, he’s just trying to push our buttons. You know him,” said Mom.

“Are you late because of me?” Zara asked.

“We’re on time. We’re not late,” said Mom shortly. “Run along now, and go to your class.”

Zara knew Mom and Dad wanted to say more about Mr Boyle but didn’t want her to hear. She walked as fast as she could to her class, which was in the middle school building. Pixie and Mimi would probably be there. Both Pixie’s parents were doctors, and Mimi’s worked in a bank, so they were dropped early.

Pixie and Mimi had been her friends from the time they had all joined the school, in kindergarten. Pixie's real name was Priyadarshini, while Mimi's was Mariam. Just as she expected, both girls were already in the classroom.

"Hi, Zara. You don't look too happy today," said Pixie. The name really suited her. She had big eyes and a little pointed chin, just like a pixie's.

"Is anything the matter?" Mimi asked. She wore small, round, Gandhi glasses that gave her a serious, scholarly look, although she was lots of fun. Zara was so glad she had such good, loyal friends. When she'd been admitted to hospital, they had talked to her every single day, telling her about school. None of the doctors could say why Zara had suddenly lost her sight, but her friends never let her feel sad at what had happened. Zara could tell them everything.

"Yes," she said, in response to Mimi's question. "I heard some very bad news." She told them of the visit to the doctor and what he said.

"I don't know how my Mom and Dad will

get fifty lakhs. We're not that rich. And if I don't have the surgery within three months, I'll become blind. That's what the doc said." Her face clouded. "The worst thing is, if I go blind, I may have to go to a special school."

Mimi and Pixie hugged her. "No, Zara, that won't happen. The school itself won't allow that to happen," said Pixie. "You're the one who's been chosen to represent our school in the science quiz."

"Pixie's right," said Mimi. "And if you and Ramu bring back the cup to the school—wow! They wouldn't want to lose a student like you."

Zara smiled. What encouraging friends she had. She was so lucky. Ramu was her partner in the science quiz, and in a higher grade. He and Zara had been chosen to represent their school in a very prestigious quiz held every year, where students from all over the country, and even abroad, participated.

Mimi scratched her head, thinking. "Zara, there are so many people who help out. Like millionaires who are waiting to help children. Philli—philo—I can't remember the word."

"Philanthropists," completed Pixie. She always did well in her English vocabulary tests. "Yes, Zara, tell your dad to contact a millionaire."

"There's something called crowd-funding too," said Mimi. "I hear my dad talking about it. It's like you make an appeal in the paper and many people send money. As much as they can afford."

"I know," sighed Zara. "But crowd-funding is different. It's for projects or business investments. Dad will have to make an appeal in the paper. And you don't know my dad. He doesn't like asking anyone for help."

"Your dad is the best teacher in the school," said Mimi. "My big sister can't stop praising him. He knows how to explain complicated things in a simple way. That's what she says."

"Yes, Zara," joined in Pixie. "He's the only teacher with a PhD. He used to practically run the school when Mr Dimpleby was headmaster. It was as if he were the Deputy Headmaster. I'm sure the school management or the new headmaster will help him get the money."

A cloud passed over Zara's face. "Well, Mr Dimpleby's gone, and now it's Mr Boyle. I don't think he'll help."

"Mr Boiled Egg," said Pixie, and the three girls giggled. They didn't want to be disrespectful, but then, nobody liked Mr Boyle much. Learning was no longer fun with him around.

"He really does look like a boiled egg wearing a suit," said Mimi. "I liked Mr Dimpleby much better."

Zara wondered if she could share more with her best friends. She decided she could. What were best friends for? "Promise you won't tell anyone? Not even your parents or your brothers or sisters?"

"Cross my heart," said both the girls. They loved secrets.

"Well," said Zara, "Mr Boyle doesn't like my Dad at all. He's not giving him any responsibilities. Dad used to also oversee the school accounts earlier, but Mr Boyle has taken away that job from him. He knew how much was being spent on school supplies. And Dad says he knows why Mr Boyle hates him."

"Why?" Both Mimi and Pixie were intrigued.

"Dad was supposed to take charge as headmaster after Mr Dimpleby left. But out of the blue, Mr Boyle assumed that position. No one knows how or why. That's why Dad says Mr Boyle doesn't like him, because he thinks he's a threat. So you see, I don't think Mr Boyle will help Dad in any way. But I'll tell him your ideas about crowd-funding or asking a philanthropist."

Both girls looked at her sadly. "Is that so?" Pixie said. "Oh, I wish either Mr Dimpleby returns, or your dad is made headmaster. Everything here has become so hard ever since Mr Boyle took over. I don't much like school anymore."

"I don't know why we have tests every week," said Mimi." School's no longer any fun."

"Don't worry, Zara," said Pixie, giving her a hug. "Your dad's so clever. He'll find a way."

Some of the other children trooped into class, and the girls stopped talking.

"Uh-oh," said Mimi, "we haven't gone to the loo yet. Let's run there. Mr Solomon will be so cross if we tell him we want to go in the middle of the class."

The three friends went as quickly as they could to the washroom, and returned in time for Mr Solomon's science class. Science was Zara's favourite subject. She still hadn't told them about Joom. Somehow, she felt it was not right to tell them unless she herself was sure. She was beginning to doubt the whole episode herself. *Was it just a dream or did Joom really exist*?

◆◆◆

Chapter 5

A Sad Day for Dad

School was over for the day. Dad drove home with a long face, concentrating on the traffic, not uttering a word. None of the usual cheerful chatter. Mom and Zara exchanged glances.

"Is anything the matter?" Mom sounded very concerned.

Dad didn't answer.

"Dad, did Mr Boyle say anything?" Zara asked. "Did he shout at you because you were late?"

Dad laughed mirthlessly. "Of course not. I'm not a student to be shouted at."

Mom turned around and gave Zara a warning look. She was seated next to Dad, with Zara sitting behind. Beside Zara lay her school bag and a big stack of notebooks that Mom was taking home to correct. This was her usual routine.

"How's your science quiz practise?" Mom asked, purposely changing the topic.

"It's fine, Mom," said Zara. She felt bad for her father. Why was he so sad and sullen? He was never moody, and usually hummed a song or asked them about their day and told them about his too. She had to put him in a good mood, somehow.

"Dad, none of the students like Mr Boyle. They all wish Mr Dimpleby had never left."

"Well, that doesn't help much," said Dad. "He's here, as headmaster. We can't change that."

"You should have been headmaster," said Mom. "I don't know how he suddenly entered the picture."

"*Pfft*," said Dad. "I don't really care that I haven't been made headmaster." He slowed down when the traffic lights turned yellow, and then stopped. He was a careful driver and had never had an accident. It was a junction, so the lights remained red for long. He was quiet for a minute, and then said, "Boyle is out to get me."

"Did he say anything?" Mom asked.

The lights turned green. Dad remained silent, concentrating on the road. Another few minutes and they'd reach home, their small two-bedroom flat in the suburb of Dwarka. They stayed in the older part of the suburb, a large, crumbling building in dire need of a coat of paint, not in one of the flashy new skyscrapers that had sprung up almost overnight.

"He knows you're more popular," continued Mom. "All the staff love you, like they loved Mr Dimpleby. That's why he resents you."

"Doesn't help much, does it?" Dad wryly remarked.

"Dad, Mom, all the students also don't like Mr Boyle because he's made everything so hard, with tests every week. It's just studies, studies, studies all the time."

Both her parents were quiet. She knew why. It was their policy not to directly say anything bad about any teacher, even a horrible one like Mr Boyle.

"And you know something else?" Zara said. "Mr Boyle looks like a big boiled egg wearing a suit. We call him Mr Hard-boiled Egg."

Zara saw in the mirror a small

smile playing at the corner of Dad's mouth. Then, he broke out into a big smile. Mom's shoulders were shaking with laughter.

"You are such bad children," she said, but Zara knew she didn't mean it. She once more turned to her husband and said, "Sameer, what's biting you? What happened?"

Again, Dad was quiet. Then he said, "Well, you might as well know. Boyle is cutting half a day's pay from my salary."

"Whatever for?" Mom's voice was high with surprise and anger.

"It seems I'm setting a bad precedent by taking half a day's leave."

"Half a day's leave? But, you had to take Zara to the doctor. Doesn't he know how important that visit was? And you're allowed to take some days off. What about the number of times you've stayed back to complete some work? You don't get paid overtime for that!" Mom spoke in a high, shaky voice.

"Dad, you needn't have come. Mom could have taken me!" Zara was sad, angry and also guilty. It was because of her that her father had to go through all this.

"Quiet!" Mom said sharply. "No one asked you for your opinion." By that time, they had reached home, and Dad parked the car. They did not get out but continued sitting. "Sameer, we have to go every two weeks to this specialist until she can have her operation. You know that. Do you mean to say that he'll cut your pay each time you go?"

"That's what he plans," said Dad.

"But he can't!"

"Yes, he can. He can do anything!"

"You can't take this lying down, Sameer. Fight back. Complain to the school board."

Dad did not answer. He switched off the ignition.

"Dad, you needn't come. I can go with Mom." Why, oh why did this happen to her, suddenly losing her vision? How she hated her life.

"Enough of this," said Dad, opening his door. "I will take my daughter every two weeks even if he cuts a whole day's pay. This is important to all of us."

"He may cut my pay too," said Mom.

"No, he said he would spare you, and that a child needed her mother when visiting the doctor. He was pretending to be very kind and considerate." Dad's lips curved upward into a horrible smilc. He walked into the building with his briefcase, forgetting to offer to carry Mom's pile of notebooks, something he did every day.

Mom and Zara followed him up the stairs to their first-floor flat, their hearts heavy.

◆◆◆

Chapter 6

Joom Again, Joom Again, Jiggery-Jag

The Kumar household was unusually quiet that evening. Dad had his dinner and then immediately shut himself in his study. He usually helped Mom with the dishes, and then the two of them watched TV for a while before going to bed. But not today.

Zara finished her homework, learnt a few questions for the science quiz (Mr Solomon had given her a *Tell Me Why* science book all about the animal world, with questions after each chapter), and then went to bed. She closed her eyes but didn't go to sleep. She waited until she heard her parents go to bed, and then waited a little longer.

The house was quiet. Reaching out for her glasses that were lying on the bedside table, she glanced at the clock with the luminous dial. 11 pm!

Perhaps Joom was waiting for her?

She crept out into her balcony. It was her own special balcony, as only her bedroom opened out onto it. So, it was like her own private green room. *Would the genie be there*? she wondered. Or had she dreamt it all up, that meeting last night?

"I thought you wouldn't come, little human," said the same sore-throaty voice. "You look even sadder today. Tell me what happened."

"I'm so glad you're here, Joom," said Zara. "I almost thought I dreamt you up."

"I'm here, little girl. Larger than life." He gave a smile that stretched from ear to ear. This time Zara could see clearly because she'd worn her glasses.

"Now," said Joom, spreading himself out with his

back resting against the wall. "Tell me, how was your day?"

Zara told him all that had happened, and how nasty Mr Boyle had cut her father's pay.

"Hmmm," said Joom, scratching his big stomach. "It must be so hard on your parents."

"And I told my best friends, Pixie and Mimi, about how my Dad needed fifty lakhs for this entire thing—the trip, the stay and the operation, along with all the medical bills. He's planning to sell my great-grandfather's house, which has been in my family for over a hundred years."

"Look, little Zara," said Joom. "Miracles do happen. Your parents will find a way of taking you to this Boss Danglies place. I've lived for over two thousand years, and I know some things better than you. And I can see into your heart, and see how pure it is."

"Is that so?" Zara asked, her eyes shining. "I even told Dad about Mimi's idea that we should ask a millionaire for help, but he wasn't very happy about it. Dad's a very proud man. He told me to leave money issues to the grown-ups."

Joom looked at her with sad eyes. "Little Zara, I don't have any magic left in me, otherwise I'd have whisked you off to Boss Danglies. And also given you a sack of gold pieces. But I know what can cheer you up a bit." He gave a big, goofy smile. "Forgotten? We made a pack last night."

"A pact," corrected Zara. "Of course, Joom. I love stories."

"Well," said Joom, settling further back against the wall. "Let me begin."

◆◆◆

Chapter 7

Joom's Story

Joom stretched out his legs and made himself more comfortable. He blended in with the shadow of the tamarind tree so that even if Mom and Dad came out, they would not see anything unusual. Zara settled herself opposite him, her toes touching his big feet.

"Once upon a time, over two thousand years ago, I was a very young genie and lived in the city of Petra. Heard of Petra?"

"Of course. It's an ancient city in Jordan. Mrs Abraham, our history teacher, told us all about it."

"Well," went on Joom. "I loved living in Petra, especially because my master, Abu Moosa, was a very kind man. He was a farmer, and grew figs and olives and owned many grape orchards. He'd found me in a stone urn, and treated me very well.

I was young and innocent, and I'd sometimes do the wrong thing, but he never lost his temper with me."

"Like what did you sometimes do wrong?"

"Oh, once he told me to milk the goats because his servants were busy picking grapes in the orchards. I did so, collecting the milk in big, silver buckets, and the smell was so delicious that I drank it all up. When he asked for the milk to make goat cheese, I didn't have any."

"Oh dear! that would make anyone angry."

"Well, not my master. I told him the truth.

I mean, I couldn't hide it because my stomach had suddenly become so big that I had difficulty just walking."

Zara laughed and laughed when Joom began walking around like a drunkard, sticking out his belly. He plonked down and continued his story.

"Well, my master merely told me that in future, I should never milk the goats before my lunch. He knew I was a young genie and needed plenty of food, and he also knew I loved goat milk and cheese. And because he was so kind to me and didn't beat me, I never again repeated that

mistake. Of course, I made lots of other mistakes. But I never stole food or ate what I harvested or milked. I knew my master would always give me enough and more food."

"What a nice master. He's just like my English teacher, Miss Ottie D'Souza. She tells us so many interesting stories, and never scolds us."

"Is that so?" Joom smiled. "Somehow, I never learnt to do proper magic, like the things genies are supposed to do, and then, even the little magic I could do, stopped." Joom became quiet, and looked sad and scared. "Now, after all these years, I can't do any magic at all, not even make a mouse appear." His voice had gone down to a barely-audible whisper. Then, as if pulling himself together, he forced a smile on his face and went on, "Except armpit farts, and that's no magic."

"Armpit farts?" Zara laughed. "How do you do armpit farts?"

"Like this," said Joom. "Put your right hand under your left armpit, and keep flapping your left arm." He began flapping his arm up and down, up and down, and Zara doubled up with laughter. *Phut! Phut! Phut! Phut!* Joom continued, getting louder and louder, and the fart sounds increasing in tempo and volume. Zara was holding her stomach and laughing away.

Suddenly, Joom stopped. He pushed himself further against the wall, blending in with the dark shadow of the tamarind tree. Zara heard her parents entering her bedroom. Quick as a hare, she jumped up—but it was too late.

"What on earth are you doing here at this time of night in the balcony?" Mom asked. "Are you talking to yourself? I heard some noises. Like some explosions."

"Mom, I came out to feel the nice cool air," said Zara. "The room was getting stuffy. And those explosions must be the tamarind pods falling to the ground." She had never lied to her parents, but she couldn't possibly tell them she was talking to a genie.

"Come in now," said Dad, "and get to bed."

"No wonder you can't get up in the

mornings," said Mom. Zara knew they were very

worried about her. After she had been tucked

into bed, she heard Mom and Dad talking about her in low voices.

"The poor girl is really sad and worried." Dad's deep voice came to her clearly.

"Why don't you ask for help? Like what Zara said—ask a millionaire for money?" Mom asked.

"It's not easy. I've asked around, and even approached the papers. They'll make an appeal on our behalf if they think the cause is worthy enough. The thing is, there are so many others who also need help. The editor told me there are two or three cases of children with leukaemia."

"Well, we have to find a way fast. Time's running out. Let's sleep. Tomorrow, there's assembly for the whole school."

Dad groaned. "Wonder what Boyle's got up his sleeve for me?"

There was quiet for a few minutes and then the sound of gentle snoring. Zara too fell asleep.

◆◆◆

Chapter 8

The Headmaster's Pet

"Good morning, boys and girls, and our respected teachers," said Mr Boyle, smiling benignly; the assembly was a weekly affair for the middle and high school students, from grades 6 to 12. Attendance was compulsory, even for the teachers. "Now, will you all please stand? We will sing the school anthem."

Zara stood up with all the other children from her class. The teachers' chairs were to one side, and Zara saw Mom and Dad also stand. The assembly was a much-dreaded ritual as Mr Boyle usually used this as an occasion to put down anyone he chose, or those who had knowingly or unknowingly offended him.

No one was spared, except of course the students whose parents had made huge donations to the school. *Who was in for it this time?* wondered Zara. She hoped it wasn't Mom and Dad, who both looked nervous and uncomfortable. Earlier, he had humiliated Miss Rita Fonseca, who had recently been hired as a substitute teacher.

Miss Fonseca had just graduated from the teacher training institute, and had a fresh, innocent bearing. Mr Boyle, pretending he didn't know her, had called her up on stage. Poor Miss Fonseca had gone up, thinking she was being introduced to the school because she was new.

"So, are you in grade 11 or 12?" Mr Boyle had asked in seeming innocence.

"Sir?" She hadn't understood.

"You're new, aren't you? Can you tell us your name and what school you've come from?"

"Mr Boyle, I'm not a student," said poor Miss Fonseca, her face going red. "I'm the substitute teacher."

Mr Boyle had clapped his hand over his mouth in mock surprise, and profusely apologised, "I'm sorry, Miss Fonseca," he said. "I really thought you were a new student." How the entire assembly had laughed at poor Miss Fonseca, who walked back red-faced.

Mr Boyle had introduced a new tradition at assembly, of a student speaking on important topics like 'Character and Success', 'Self-Discipline is the Best Discipline', 'Health is Wealth', and so on.

There was a small murmur of surprise in the auditorium as a muscular-looking boy with well-developed biceps and the beginnings of a moustache sauntered up on to the stage. It was the notorious Adam Butt, the biggest bully in

the school. Everyone, especially the younger children, avoided Adam Butt and his bunch of rowdy boys. He was known to have grabbed lunch-boxes, spat into them and then handed them back with a big smile on his face.

Or else, if someone's mother had packed a special treat like a chocolate bar or a slice of cake, he would eat it noisily and then toss the box back to the kid. While Mr Dimpleby was headmaster, he had not dared to misbehave. But now it was a different story. Zara heard how he bullied the more timid boys, threatened them to do his homework, and (she overheard Dad talking about this to Mom), was even caught smoking in the toilets.

Sometimes, the boys lay in wait for whoever they could harass after school, pouncing on them and demanding money. Not that Adam Butt needed money. He was the wealthiest boy in school, and his father had made an enormous donation for the new school auditorium. Which was why he was Mr Boyle's favourite.

"That boy ought to be expelled," Dad said. "He's setting a bad precedent."

"Ha! You got a hope," replied Mom. "Seems his father's opened a new factory too. How can such an important personage be expelled?"

Adam Butt began reading his topic, "Our respected headmaster, teachers and friends, today my topic is, 'Try, try and try again until you succeed'". Zara saw some of the boys in his class snigger. Adam was the laziest boy who scraped through because he had a battery of tutors who worked hard with him at home just before the exams. He gave the meek-willed teachers a rough time by openly confronting them, so they decided to leave him well alone.

He and his rowdy friends would sit at the back of the class, looking through some magazines or playing games on their mobile phones. Only an experienced and firm teacher like Dr Sameer, Zara's father, knew how to deal with him, setting him different sums and making him sit in the front row of the classroom. None of his teachers liked him, but he was Mr Boyle's pet, his favourite. Whenever he passed by, he'd chuff Adam under the chin and ask after his father.

Adam Butt repeated, "Our most respected head-master, teachers and friends, today my topic is 'Try, try and try again until you succeed'."

Adam began scratching his head, having forgotten the next line, and then looked down at his paper. He then proceeded to read out the entire speech. He droned on, making many errors while reading. He read one of the paragraphs twice over, and instead of saying, 'We should not be weak-kneed people', he said, 'we should not be weak-peed people.'

He ended his speech. Mr Boyle gave a big smile and patted him on his back.

"Adam Butt, that was an excellent speech. Will all of you clap for him?"

No one was ever asked to clap after an

assembly speech, but the students dutifully obeyed, and his friends let out whoops.

"Now," said Mr Boyle, looking very pleased. "You must be as clear and concise as this young man when making a speech. You may all go now."

Assembly was dismissed. The students got up to leave when suddenly Mr Boyle put his hand up and said, "Stop."

Everyone stopped in their tracks, silent, wondering why. Even Adam Butt looked surprised. And then they heard it. A snore.

◆◆◆

Chapter 9

The Snoring Boy

It was not a big snore but a gentle snore, like the ones people make while dozing off after a heavy afternoon lunch. The entire school remained silent, listening to the snores.

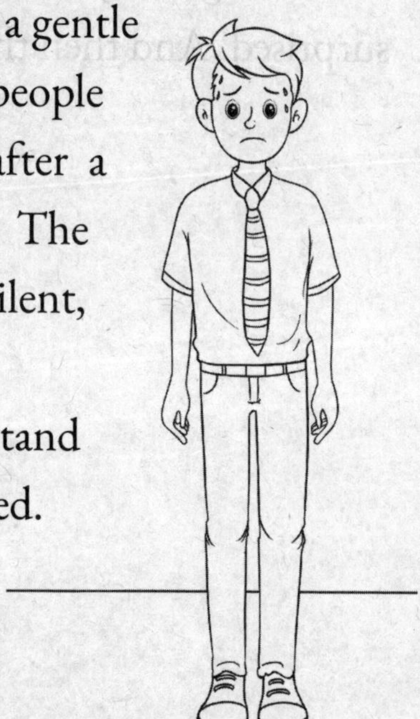

"Dickie Douglas, stand up!" his class teacher roared.

Dickie—a clumsy-looking boy who had big ears and big

hands and feet and a frightened look on his face—slowly rose.

"Come here, boy," said Mr Boyle very softly.

The entire assembly shuddered. Zara especially felt her stomach turn somersaults. When Mr Boyle spoke softly, he meant business. She and the other students watched in fascinated horror as Dickie walked to the stage.

"Now boy, what is your name? Come and stand here."

"Dickie Douglas, sir," said poor Dickie, and went and stood in front of the mike beside Mr Boyle. Adam Butt had returned to his seat.

"You know we take the assembly sessions very seriously here, don't you?" Mr Boyle said. "Assembly time is sacrosanct." Mr Boyle loved using big words like this to impress the students. Zara remembered him using the word 'lackadaisical' and had later asked Dad what it meant.

"Without any enthusiasm," Dad explained, and then added that one needed to carry a dictionary when talking to Mr Boyle.

"Yes, sir. I'm sorry, sir. It was my mom's birthday yesterday and I went to bed very late. That's why I fell asleep." Poor Dickie's voice came out very low.

"Mom's birthday, eh?" Mr Boyle gave another smile. "Too much cake, eh?"

Dickie remained quiet, but his hands were trembling.

"Okay, Dickie-boy, since you enjoyed yourself so much last night, I want our students too to have some fun."

Dickie gulped. What did Mr Boyle have in store for him? The students also waited, holding their breath.

"Close your eyes, boy, and snore. I want you to snore for a whole minute."

"Sir?" Dickie was incredulous.

"You heard me, boy. Don't waste my time and everybody else's time. Begin."

Poor Dickie. Zara felt so bad for him. He let out two small snores like little grunts, and then stopped.

"I said one minute," said Mr Boyle ever so softly. "I am timing you."

Dickie closed his eyes once more and began making snoring noises. After a few grunts, everyone started laughing, and by the end of the minute, the entire assembly was roaring with laughter. Except for the teachers and some students. Zara exchanged glances with Mimi and Pixie, who also looked appalled.

"Poor Dickie," whispered Mimi.

"He's so humiliated, he's crying now," said Pixie.

Dickie walked back to his seat, head down. Zara wanted to go up to him, tell him exactly what she thought of Mr Boyle and his meanness, tell him that not everyone found this funny but

were angry at what was done to him. The laughter stopped. There was a hushed silence. But no one dared open their mouth to give Dickie any words of sympathy.

"Remember, boys and girls," said Mr Boyle, before dismissing the meeting. "Assembly time is sacrosanct. I wish you all a very good day."

The students first left, followed by the teachers. Dickie Douglas was trailing behind all the other students. Zara saw Dad wait for him, pat him on the back and say some words to him. Dickie's expression changed a little, and he stopped crying. Then Zara saw the black-suited figure of Mr Boyle watching Dad and Dickie with ill-concealed hatred. Her heart missed a beat.

◆◆◆

Chapter 10

Joom Bungles Up

Later that night, Zara told Joom all about how Mr Boyle had been nasty to Dickie Douglas.

"Mr Boyle's horrid not just to students but to teachers too. I overheard Mom and Dad talking about him," she told Joom. "And he saw my Dad speaking to Dickie when they were returning to class. I'm sure Dad told him something comforting. But Mr Boyle saw them talking. I don't know what he's going to do to Dad. Maybe it's his turn at the next assembly."

"Dearie me," said Joom, like an old grandmother. "So, even human beings can have bad bosses. I thought only genies could get bad masters."

"My Dad's the best teacher," said Zara proudly. "That's why Mr Boyle doesn't like him. And he cares so much for me. He said even if Mr Boyle cuts his pay each day that he comes with me to the doctor's, he'll still come. He'd never leave me and Mom to go through all this alone."

"You're lucky, little human, to have such a nice father."

Zara responded by giving Joom a big hug. She couldn't reach all the way round him, but hugged whatever bit of him she could reach. "Thank you, Joom. I'm so happy you're my friend."

"Me too," said Joom.

"Can you tell me another story? Maybe a funny one?"

"Hmmm. Let me think. There were so many silly things I did for my first master, and he never

beat me." He scratched his head. Zara could hear the *krrrr krrrr krrrr* of his nails on his scalp. "Ah, yes, this mistake was quite funny, but it worked out well in the end. My first master, Abu Moosa, told me to make a bouquet of big white flowers and tie them up with a beautiful red bow for a birthday party, which he had to attend that evening. It seems the lady, a very special friend of his, loved white flowers. I could do a bit of magic in those days. Not much, but just a bit.

"So I said, *Abracadabra, phoo-bee-hee*
Get me the rarest of flowers you can see.
Tie the bunch up with a bow of red silk
And paint the flowers as white as milk.

"Well, my magic created a beautiful big bunch of white flowers with green petals and long, green stalks. They didn't smell very nice but then, Master Moosa hadn't told me he wanted fragrant flowers, so I wasn't very worried. He was all dressed up that evening and asked me for the flowers. I brought them out. And then, instead of thanking me for giving him a bouquet of the rarest and most beautiful flowers in the world, he just stared at them.

"Then he said, 'Joom, do you know the name of this flower?'

"'No, master, I don't. But you had told me to bring you a bunch of rare flowers, so that's what I did. I didn't want to give you lilies or white roses because they are so common.'

"Master Moosa just stared at me, and then started laughing. He laughed and laughed so much that tears began rolling down his cheeks. 'Master, did I do something wrong?' I asked him. 'You buffoon, these are not rare flowers. They are heads of a cauliflower.' Cauliflower? I hadn't heard of such a word. 'It's a vegetable, you little noodle-doodle!' Even though I'd made such a big mistake, Master Moosa never used any bad words or swore at me to make me feel bad."

"Then did you make a new bouquet for him?" Zara asked, laughing away.

"No, I couldn't. At that time, I could do only one magic a day. So, Master Moosa had to take that bouquet to his friend's party. But you know what?"

"What?"

"When he came back late at night, and I'd brought him his night-robe and his slippers, he told me, 'Joom, you may be a noodle-doodle, but your mistakes always turn out well. My friend, Lady Popeen, loves cauliflower because she rarely gets to eat it. So, she thought this was the best and most unique gift of all.'"

Both Joom and Zara chuckled. Zara felt so much better talking to Joom.

"Can you still do a teensy-weensy bit of magic?" Zara asked.

The genie's face fell, and all the little lines on

his forehead and cheeks drooped down. "No, not any more. I've lost all my magic."

He looked so forlorn that Zara patted him.

"You know, Joom, you may not be the cleverest or the most powerful of genies, but you have a special gift, of making people happy. And that's the best gift of all."

"Is that so, little human?" Joom asked. "Master Moosa used to tell me the same thing. But now, it's one o' clock. If you don't go to bed, you'll never be able to get up in the morning. So, good night, human child, and I'll see you tomorrow night."

"Goodnight, Joom," said Zara, and crept back quietly to her bedroom.

If it were not for Joom, how would she have spent her nights? Just feeling sad, she knew. But Joom had brought so much love and laughter to her life that she forgot about all her big problems.

◆◆◆

Chapter 11

What's Up Now?

Two weeks went by, and Zara had to once again visit the special doctor. Despite Mom saying she could manage to take Zara on her own, Dad had insisted on coming. "It's my daughter's eyes, and her future. I'm not missing any classes. Boyle knows that all too well." Zara was glad that he was accompanying them. She felt so much more confident when they were both with her.

This time, the doctor squirted some cold liquid into her eyes and looked at them through a huge magnifying glass. And then, she had to look at different pictures and colours and letters

of the alphabet through another device, with her head angled on a cold, hard metal bar. It was like what one normally goes through at an optician's when you are testing your power or getting new glasses. Only this took so much longer. It hadn't hurt, but Zara had to keep still for so long that her back and neck were sore.

They returned to school just as the bell rang for the lunch break.

"You better have lunch with us in Dad's office," said Mom. "And rest a bit. Then you can go to class."

"Okay, Mom," said Zara. For once, she didn't argue because, to be honest, she was a bit tired. Otherwise, she would have insisted on joining Pixie and Mimi in the playground.

Dad's office was the biggest in the school. It was only a little smaller than Mr Boyle's office. Mr Dimpleby had given him this room on account of his seniority, and Zara had overheard Dad tell Mom that Mr Boyle was planning to move him to a smaller office that he'd have to share with some of the other teaching staff.

Dad's room would be used for 'other purposes' (although he never actually spelt out what those 'other purposes' were). But Mr Boyle hadn't yet got round to doing it. Mom didn't have an office to herself but shared a room with other members of the teaching staff.

Zara loved Dad's office. She rarely went there except when Dad had to stay back after school hours. Then, she and Mom would wait for him in his office to finish his meeting, and Zara would complete her homework while her mother would prepare for the next day's class. Or else, they'd play a fun game like capitals of countries.

Dad's office smelt of Dad, a smell of coffee and air-freshener, and in Zara's imagination, of math sums doing somersaults and playing around. There was a bookshelf with all kinds of math books, some of them old and dog-eared, many copies of the *Mathematics* magazine that she loved flicking through, and a blackboard with chalk-pieces.

Zara once asked her father why he didn't have a whiteboard like in the classrooms. "Dad, people haven't even heard of a blackboard. That was used in the last century," she said.

Her father chuckled. "I learnt all my math through a blackboard, and with pen and paper and no calculator," he said. "I think those kids who come to my office to sort out their confusion about some principle enjoy writing on a blackboard and using chalk to work out equations." It was true what he said. Zara practiced sums on the blackboard, and even drew things on it when she was bored. Once, she and Mom had played a game of tic-tac-toe when waiting for Dad.

Dad's desk faced the door, and his pens, pencils, rulers, and mathematical instruments were laid out in a neat row, the spaces between each item arranged with mathematical precision. This was a room that belonged to a math teacher. Everything clean, orderly, not a speck of dust anywhere, and every item in its place.

The one item that seemed out of place was a comfortable-looking old sofa placed in a corner of the room. Dad sometimes relaxed on this sofa when he had to stay back after school to attend a very late meeting with the board. It was easier than driving all the way back home and then returning, what with all the traffic.

Like last time, the doctor had once again told her parents that they had only three months to save her sight (again when he thought she was out of earshot and seated in the adjacent room). Dad and Mom had looked grim. Only Zara, thinking of Joom's words, that there would be a way, was not so despondent. Somehow, she believed in Joom. The family had just finished eating their cheese and tomato sandwiches when there was a knock on the door. "Dr Sameer, the headmaster wants to see you." It was Gagan, Mr Boyle's office assistant.

Zara saw her father look up in surprise. "Now?"

"Yes, sir. He said it's urgent."

Mom and Dad exchanged worried looks.

"This won't take long," he told them. "It must be about the math quiz." He left the room, closing the door behind him.

◆◆◆

Chapter 12

Some Shocking News

Zara sat up straight as soon as the door closed. Her heart was beating fast. Her eyes met her mother's, who looked just as disturbed.

"Mom, why has Mr Boyle called Dad? I thought you said he never involved him in anything. Why suddenly?" Zara was as surprised as her parents.

"I have no idea," said Mom.

"Maybe he's going to tell Dad that it's ok, he won't cut his pay?" Zara said. "The whole school knows how sincere he is."

Mom shrugged. Then, giving Zara a stern look, she said, "OK, young lady, go and lie on the sofa and take some rest. You do want to pay attention during the afternoon lessons, don't you, and not fall asleep in class? Now, no more arguments. I'll wake you up five minutes before the lunch break ends."

Zara gave a grin and went to lie down on the sofa. She knew when to argue, when not to. The sofa was an old one, with an indentation in the middle, and covered with a soft velvet fabric in faded maroon. When Zara lay down on it, she found herself sinking into the indentation. It was so comfortable that she fell asleep almost immediately. But not for long.

"Boyle wants me out." Dad had returned to the room.

"What?" Mom's voice was shrill.

"Seems there's been a serious complaint against me by one of the students' fathers. It seems I humiliated the boy in front of the whole class and purposely failed him in the final test, so he can't take up Higher Math next year."

"No," said Mom. "No, you would never do that. Who's the boy?"

"Adam Butt Chaudhury. His father said I shouted at him so badly that he failed the test."

Zara sat up. "Adam Butt Chaudhury is the biggest liar. Everybody knows that."

"Go back to sleep," Mom said sharply.

"No, Mom. I won't," said Zara. "He's the biggest bully in the school."

Dad sat down heavily. Zara saw that his face had become white. Mom's too.

"It's a water-tight case," said Dad. "It seems all the students in the class have signed a petition swearing that I yelled at him for no reason and stopped him from writing the exam."

"What?" Mom sounded disbelieving. "No, it's a plot to get you out."

Dad went on as if he hadn't heard Mom. "Boyle told me that the school board wants me to

go immediately, especially because Adam's father has given such a huge donation this year. Boyle said he could do nothing about it and promised he'd pay me all my dues."

Tears were streaming down Mom's face. "No, they can't do this to you. You have to fight back."

Zara walked up to her father and put her hand on his shoulder. "Dad, you're the best teacher in the school. They can't tell you to go. There's been some horrible mistake. You have to fight back, like Mom said."

Dad patted Zara. "Go and lie down. I'm sorry that you have to hear all this." Then, turning to his wife, he said, "I can't fight. The case against me is too strong."

Knock! Knock! There was a sharp rap on the door. Who could it be? Zara went back to the couch and lay down. Maybe it was Mr Boyle who had come to apologise and tell Dad it was all a mistake.

"Come in," said Dad.

The door opened.

◆◆◆

Chapter 13

Mr Solomon Spills the Beans

Zara lay back on the sofa, her glasses still perched on her nose. She closed her eyes, but opened them just a teeny-weeny crack. Who was it knocking on the door? Mr Solomon! Zara watched the lanky form of her science teacher with his mass of black, curly hair. She gave a small smile.

Ramu had nicknamed him the 'mad scientist' and indeed, with his wild hair and absent-minded looks, he resembled a young Albert Einstein. "Mad science teachers are the best," Ramu had

pronounced, and Zara couldn't but agree. Mr Solomon's classes were the most fun.

He allowed his students to perform experiments, pouring one liquid into another (of course under strict supervision), explaining the scientific principles behind myths (like why do we say 'once in a blue moon'), and even teaching the class how to make stink bombs. That stink-bomb class had been the best ever.

But what was Mr Solomon doing here? He was Dad's best friend, but he never visited him during school hours. Zara watched his skinny form as he seated himself opposite Dad.

"I've got something to tell you," he said.

"I know. Boyle's fired me. I just got the news."

"Yes, I know you must have been told that. It's grossly unfair. But I have something more to tell you." He glanced behind him nervously.

"Nobody's going to come," said Dad. "Boyle left early, after firing me."

"Right," said Mr Solomon. "Well, I never had time to meet you this week, but there's something you must know."

Dad looked at him. "What else do I need to know?" he asked dryly.

"Should I leave the room?" Mom asked.

"No, ma'am, please stay. This concerns you as much as it does your husband."

Zara saw Mom and Dad look at each other in alarm. She lay on the couch as quiet as a mouse. Mr Solomon hadn't seen her, and her parents seemed to have forgotten she was present in the room.

"I was going into Boyle's office when Gagan told me that Boyle was expecting an important guest and I had to wait."

"When was this?" Zara saw Dad put both his elbows on his table, and bring one hand under his chin.

"Sometime last week. Say six or seven days ago. I waited at the little reception adjoining Mr Boyle's office, and I saw the important guest enter. It was Adam Butt's father, Mr Chaudhury."

"Hmmm," Mom snorted. "The Butt boy is the one who's created all the trouble. I know the father made an enormous donation to the school for the new hall. Something like twenty lakh rupees."

Mr Solomon nodded, his black mass of curls bobbing up and down.

"Gagan was all smiles and held the door open for him. He then left on some errand, and I was sitting alone in that room. I expected the important guest to leave soon." Mr Solomon drummed the table with his long, bony fingers, a habit that Zara and her classmates were familiar with. She slightly shifted her head so she could hear better. "Well, this Mr Chaudhury, Adam Butt's father, seemed furious. He stomped into the office. I could hear Mr Boyle greet him warmly. But he didn't return the greeting. He seemed mad."

"How did you know all this when the door was shut?" Dad asked.

Mr Solomon grinned. "Well, the door was ajar. I could hear every single word as clearly as if I were sitting in that same room." He paused, and reached for the bottle of water Dad kept on his table. “May I?” he asked.

“Of course,” answered Dad. Zara could see Mom was getting a little irritated at how long the story was taking.

“Dr Sameer, you know that Mr Boyle seems to be on a mission to undo everything that you and Mr Dimpleby have done in building up this school.” Dad nodded. “But what I heard that day was totally the pits.”

“Let’s hear it,” said Dad quietly.

“Mr Chaudhury said you were creating a lot of problems for his son. It seems you purposely stopped him from writing his exam paper. So now, he won’t be able to take Higher Math in the next class.”

“The boy was cheating,” said Dad. Zara was surprised at how cool he was. “I caught him red-handed. He had his mobile phone with him, and all the programs saved on his notes. I even saw a text message to some tutoring service. How can I allow this to happen?”

"Is that so?" Mr Solomon said. "Mr Chaudhury never said anything like this."

"In fact, I gave the boy another chance. I told him to work hard and take the test again after two weeks. But obviously, he wants to take the easy way out and blame me."

"Did you say this to Mr Boyle?" Mom asked.

"Of course I did," said Dad.

"We all know how lazy that boy is," said Mr Solomon. "A month before the final exams, his father hires a whole load of tutors to get him to pass. Anyway," Mr Solomon tossed his empty bottle into the trash can, "the father told Boyle that he'd better do something about this. He wasn't giving these donations for his son to be rusticated. He said the boy is so afraid of you that he's stopped eating. His mother's very worried about him."

Despite himself, Dad smiled.

Mr Solomon went on, "The father seems to be as obnoxious as his son. He complained that you expect his son to complete his homework, and if he doesn't, he'd have to stay back after school to finish it. 'The master, Dr Sameer, expects my son to do his homework regularly. Is he a girl to study every day?' Those were his exact words."

Zara bristled when she heard this. She almost jumped up and stopped herself just in time from giving the game away. *Girls study and boys don't? Only girls are expected to do homework? What utter nonsense!* She would have liked to give that father a box on his ears.

"I know Boyle needed an excuse to throw me out. And now he's got it. The perfect reason. No one from the board is going to take my side when the father is Mr Money-bags."

Mr Solomon nodded, but Mom was going red with anger.

"And there's more," said Mr Solomon. "It seems Mr Chaudhury is opening a toilet paper factory. Luxury toilet paper. He mentioned the name too. *Butt Luxury Wipes*. He asked Boyle if he needed to order any toilet paper for the school. Mr Boyle—and I heard him clearly—said, 'Not really. But I can always change the suppliers. I'm whole and sole in charge here. But will you have something for me then?'

"He laughed and so did the father. 'No compulsion, Mr Boiled,' answered the father. 'But if you do, you won't be disappointed'."

Zara suppressed a giggle. *Butt Luxury Wipes.* Wait till she told Pixie and Mimi!

"Imagine," went on Mr Solomon, "the headmaster is taking money under the table."

"Solomon," said Dad. "What you tell me completes the puzzle. Obviously, Boyle wants me out. You know I oversee school accounts too, and know how the money's used. There's no reason to order luxury wipes for the school. We get ours from a wholesale dealer at a very low price. He wants me out so I wouldn't know of this."

"Sameer, you have to report this to the

board," said Mom. "Why are you so passive?" Zara could see she was shaking with anger.

"Report what?" Dad asked. "That Mr Solomon overheard a conversation that he shouldn't have been overhearing? And get him into trouble too? Besides, I have no solid proof. All Boyle will do is to deny it. And Mr Chaudhury too."

"Yes, but you can't take this lying down. You have to fight back. What about our Zara's operation?" Mom's voice had risen to a shriek.

"There's more to this case," said Dad calmly. "You haven't heard the whole story. It seems all the students in Adam Butt's class have signed a petition saying I am prejudiced against Adam Butt and had stopped him from writing the exam."

Zara, Mom and Mr Solomon gaped.

"When did you learn this?" Mr Solomon asked.

"Just now, when he fired me. He showed me the letter with all the signatures."

Zara could take it no longer. She got up from her reclining position. "Dad, you just have to fight back. Mom's right. Stop being such a wimp."

Mr Solomon turned in surprise when he heard her voice. "You here, Zara? I didn't see you."

"Good afternoon, Mr Solomon," said Zara.

"How's the preparation for the science quiz?"

"Going on well, sir." She was glad he had asked such a mundane question. Everyone's emotions were running high.

"I'm leaving now," said Dad. He addressed Zara and her mother. "You both take a cab home." Then, turning to Mr Solomon, he said, "You've been a good friend, Solomon. But there's nothing I can do. You better go, or else you'll be next on the list."

Dad threw a few things into his briefcase, and as he was leaving, he turned to Zara. "I'm sorry that you had to sit through all this. You're too young to be going through this. But I promise you one thing. I'll get you to Los Angeles for that operation within three months. You'll see."

Zara went and hugged her father. Dad's shoulders shook with suppressed sobs. Then, with a great effort, he straightened himself.

"Boyle wants to destroy me," he said.

"Dad, he won't. He'll never be able to destroy you," said Zara. Why should this happen to her poor, hardworking father who was doing his job honestly? Life wasn't fair.

Then she remembered Joom's words. "Dad, there's always a way out. That horrid Mr Boyle is going to be punished. Just wait and see."

Dad smiled sadly. "Let's see," he said and gave her a pat on the back and left.

◆◆◆

Chapter 14

A Sad Evening

The rest of the afternoon went by in a haze as Zara sat silent and sad in class. Pixie and Mimi, good friends that they were, thought she didn't want to talk, so they left her alone. Normally, Zara would have been excited at taking a taxi ride home, but not today. She and Mom sat quietly at the back, looking out of the window at the passing traffic. Mom leaned across and squeezed Zara's hand.

"Don't you worry, Zara. Your Dad is so clever. They can't dismiss him so easily. There must be some terrible mistake."

Zara smiled weakly. She knew Mom was trying to make her feel better. As soon as they entered their tiny apartment, Zara yelled out for her father.

"Dad, we're back."

There was no answer.

"He must be in the bathroom," said Mom, "or probably resting."

Zara pushed open her parents' bedroom door. Dad couldn't have gone very far. Their house only had a sitting-cum-dining room and two bedrooms, a medium-sized one for her parents and a small one for her. Zara loved her room because she had access to the balcony beside which grew the tamarind tree.

It was like her own private space. And Dad liked that his bedroom had a small study. It wasn't really a study but a box-room where you could keep all your suitcases and unwanted things, but Dad liked to call it his study. Dad was wide-awake on the bed, staring into space. He didn't smile at Zara or even look her way.

"Dad, are you sick? Why aren't you answering me?"

Mom just then entered. "Sameer, don't be sad. We'll find a way. You have to take this up with the board."

"Please leave me alone, you two," said Dad.

Zara saw her mother's face droop. Dad had never been so rude to her.

"You have to take it up," repeated Mom. "It's your job."

"There's no point."

"Oh, you're such a loser. You have to fight," said Mom.

And for the first time, Zara heard her gentle, mild-mannered father shout. His voice came out all rough and angry. "Fight? Fight Boyle? Fight the board? And get kicked out without my dues? How will we pay the rent? And have you forgotten Zara's operation? I need every single rupee. Do you understand, Seema, if I fight I'll get nothing." Dad's voice had increased in volume, and by the end, he was screaming. Zara was sure the neighbours could hear him. But Mom didn't seem to bother. She too shouted.

"You caught that boy cheating, and that's why you took action. Why can't you tell the board that this was what happened? You can't take this lying down."

Dad glared at her. He looked ugly, like a stranger, not like her beloved father.

"What do you mean, don't take it lying

down? Am I just half the man to you? You know Boyle has the board under his thumb. There's no point. I just have to find another job in another school. Not that that would be easy after they hear of this incident."

"But they can't do this to you," shouted Mom.

"Well, they have," said Dad. "Just thrown me out, like I'm an old pair of shoes."

"Dad, does this mean I can't have my operation and will go blind? And go to a special school?" Zara asked.

Her parents looked at her, and then at each other guiltily. Mom hugged her.

"You'll have your operation. We won't let you go blind," said Dad.

"Don't you worry your head over these problems. Go and drink your milk," said Mom.

Zara left, closing the door behind her. But she heard her father talking quietly, his voice breaking. "What will I do? Boyle's turned our lives upside-down. What can we do?"

And for once, her mother had no answers. That evening was the saddest ever in the small family. When Zara went to bed, she tossed and turned. She heard a quiet knock on her window and knew it was Joom, but she did not go out. She just lay, staring into the darkness.

◆◆◆

Chapter 15

Tough Times

The next morning, Zara and her parents set out with a heavy heart. Joom had once again knocked on her window late at night, but Zara had turned her back and pretended to be asleep. *What's the point,* she thought bitterly, *of being told that everything will be alright, when nothing can be more wrong!*

But a tiny little worm of doubt was niggling inside her. Perhaps Joom was right? That there's always a way out? But if there was a way out, why hadn't he found a solution to his problem? No, she didn't want to meet Joom and hear his silly words.

"I don't know how I'll face my colleagues," said Dad as they were nearing the school. Mom was about to say something but decided against it. Zara knew what it was. Oh why, oh why was Dad such a wimp? He was so dedicated to his profession, but he was not a fighter. That was his problem. He always let others take advantage of his goodness.

Once Zara had heard Mom constantly tell Dad that he was too non-confrontational. She hadn't known the meaning, and looked it up in the dictionary. Yes, Dad was so passive that everyone took him for granted. Dad was about to park his car in his dedicated parking slot, the one with Head of Math in big red letters on a board, when he saw another car was already parked there. The board was missing.

"Boyle hasn't wasted much time in showing me my place," he said. "I don't know why I have to come at all." He parked the car in the general parking area reserved for parents and visitors.

The small family walked in, and Zara braced herself for the day, as surely the entire school would have by now learnt that her father had been fired. And she thought of poor Dad. If it was so bad for her, how much worse it would be for him? It didn't bear thinking about.

The day passed uneventfully. The teachers gave her sympathetic looks, but she was extra quiet in class. Even when she knew the answer to a Geography question that no one else in the class knew (*Name the two tributaries of the River Nile*), she did not raise her hand. She wanted to blend in like a little grey mouse, neither be seen nor heard.

Only Mimi and Pixie, her best friends, squeezed her hand when they walked by to their seats. During the first recess, they did not go out but went and sat beside her.

"Don't be sad, Zara," said Pixie. "We heard

what happened to your dad. But the school will never find a better teacher."

Zara wished she could agree, and for a minute, she thought she'd tell them of what Mr Solomon had said, that the headmaster was firing her Dad because he didn't want him to learn about the luxury toilet paper he was going to order for the school. Then she remembered what Dad had said, that this was just 'hearsay' or something overheard, and not based on actual evidence. What was the point of telling her friends about this?

"It's a big lie what's being said about him," added Mimi. "He's the fairest teacher in the school. I don't know how those Class 10 students signed that petition."

Zara smiled at both her friends through her tears. "Thank you for supporting me," she said. "I don't know now whether I can have my operation. I mean, if my Dad's out of a job, where will we get all that money?"

"Don't you worry," said Pixie. "Your dad is so smart, he'll find another job very soon."

Zara perked up. "Do you think so?

"Of course," said both Mimi and Pixie. "A good math teacher is so hard to find. So many schools will fight to take him."

Pixie looked at her watch, a big watch she'd got for her birthday shaped like a sunflower. "There's just five minutes left before the bell rings. We'll run and use the toilet. You know how cross Mr Solomon gets when we say we want to go to the restroom."

The three girls walked as quickly as they could, Zara in the middle, to the restroom. By the time they'd finished, the bell rang. The corridors were crowded with students returning to class. And it was then that the three girls saw a group of boys laughing and talking loudly.

"Is that Dr Sameer's daughter?" they asked.

"It's her. The same. Can't you see she has the

same big nose? And look at those thick glasses she's wearing. They must be made from coke bottles." They laughed, purposely talking loudly so that Zara would hear.

The leader of the group was a tall boy with big muscles and the beginnings of a small moustache. Adam Butt and his notorious friends! It was them.

"Big Foot, come here," yelled out Adam.

From behind them came Dickie Douglas. The girls knew he was called Big Foot the Yeti or Big Ears on account of his huge feet and ears.

"See that one there," said Adam, gesturing at Zara. "Give her a dose of her father's medicine."

To Zara and the girls' horror, Dickie was holding a thin stick in his hand. He approached Zara, and she thought for a moment that he'd hit her. *Thwack!* The stick hit the ground with a loud sound and the boys jeered.

"Bravo, Big Ears," they shouted. "Gave her a good scare. Serves her right, too."

"Will you stop it?" Pixie went up to the boys.

"Stop what?" they mocked. Then, before they could say anything more, someone shouted, "Run. Old Matthew's coming." Within seconds, the gang disappeared.

Zara wished the ground would open up and swallow her.

"Zara, don't you mind. They're stupid bullies," said Mimi.

"Wipe your tears," said Pixie kindly, "or else Mr Solomon will wonder what's up."

For the millionth time, Zara thanked her lucky stars that she had two such good friends. Mr Solomon gave her an extra special smile and asked her in front of the whole class about her preparation for the science quiz. He told the entire class that they should give Zara and Ramu all the encouragement to win the quiz and cheer for them as loud as they could so they'd bring back the cup to the school. The science quiz cup had been won by other schools for the last three years.

That night, Zara wondered whether to tell her

parents about how Adam Butt had behaved with her, using Dickie, but then thought better of it. Her parents had enough problems of their own. Besides, what could they do? Dad was going. But maybe, if she won the cup for the school in the quiz, Mr Boyle would perhaps change his mind about firing Dad?

Zara finished her homework quietly that evening, prepared some more questions for the science quiz, and then went to bed. Maybe tonight, she would meet Joom? She tried to keep her eyes open to hear his knock, but was so tired that she fell asleep.

At exactly 11 pm, there was a small knock on the window.

◆◆◆

Chapter 16

A Friend in Need Is a Friend Indeed

Zara got up immediately after the second knock. Perhaps her subconscious mind was waiting for it. She hadn't met Joom for two whole nights. When she slipped outside into her balcony, she found the genie seated in his usual place, a large dark shadow against the wall.

"You don't want to be friends with me, little human?" Joom asked. "Are you angry with me?"

"How can I ever be angry with you, Joom," said Zara. "You're my BFF."

"BFF?"

"Best friend forever," explained Zara.

Joom smiled a big, happy smile. It was so easy to please him. "I'm so glad you think so," he said. "But why are you looking so sad?"

Zara's face was puffy and her hair hadn't been made into two neat plaits. Mom plaited her hair every night before she went to bed, so that it wouldn't be all knotty and tangled when she got up in the morning. But she hadn't bothered to do so for the last two days. Her forehead was knotted with worry, and she made Zara jam sandwiches for lunch instead of peanut butter, although she knew Zara didn't like jam much. But Zara quietly ate them without complaining.

"Little human," went on Joom, his wrinkly face full of concern. "I've never seen you so sad ever. Tell Joom everything."

Zara then told him the whole story. It was so nice to get it off her chest. "Those boys were so horrid to me," she said. "But I'm not too worried

about that. Pixie and Mimi are still my friends, and that's all that matters. No, Joom. It's not just bad that Dad's lost his job, but the students signing a petition accusing my dad, who has always been so just, of being unfair to this boy! Dad says it'll be hard to get a job in another school with this kind of reputation." Zara gulped back the sob. "And I'm not sure if I can ever go to Los Angeles for the operation. Everything's up in the air."

"Oh, dearie, dearie me!" Joom sighed. He hugged Zara, and she felt better immediately.

"And the inter-school science quiz is coming up soon. Do you think, Joom, that if I and Ramu win the cup for the school, Mr Boyle will change his mind about firing my dad?"

Joom thought for a moment and then said, "Why not? He can change his mind."

Zara's eyes lit up. "And Joom, I have to tell you this. I haven't even told Mom or she'll scold me, but the overall winner of this quiz, the student who gets the most answers right, will be given a special prize of two lakhs. I'm so hoping I'll get that prize. That'll really help Dad."

"Yes, little Zara, we all have our dreams. It's good to have dreams. And I hope your dream comes true."

"Thank you, Joom," said Zara. Then her face clouded over. "Joom, you always say that if your heart is pure and your intentions good, things will work out well. But I don't believe that any longer. See what's happened to Dad."

Joom remained quiet. "No, wait and see, human child, it'll get sorted out. And so will your worries over your operation. You'll see. Everything will work out well in the end."

"No, Joom," said Zara, a frown on her face. "If that were the case, what about you? You're still on the run from that evil master of yours. What was his name? Gorgonzola, wasn't it?"

"Shhh," said Joom, his eyes round with fear. "I don't want to even say his name out loud in case he's around here somewhere."

"Joom, it's just a name," said Zara. "Gorgonzola. A cheese from Italy. Not everyone likes that cheese." She stopped, as Joom was now quaking with fear.

"No, no, little one, please don't say that name. It's because of him I lost all my magic. In fact," and here all Joom's wrinkles scrunched up more, "he made me do such bad things, I don't think I can ever forgive myself."

"Oh, Joom," said Zara, "you're not bad at all. I think you're the kindest being I've ever met. And if that Mr G made you do something very bad, you couldn't help it. I mean, you're a genie and have to obey your master's commands." She didn't say Gorgonzola again as it had such a devastating effect on poor Joom.

"I know, little human," said Joom. "You're right. But I don't think I can forgive myself for the last thing I did for him." Joom sat with his big huge hand under his chin, looking pensive. Zara patted him.

"Would you like to tell me about it?" she asked. "After all, I tell you all the things that upset me, and I feel much better after that. Maybe you will too."

Joom thought for a moment. "Alright," he said, "I'll tell you everything." He settled himself down a little more comfortably. "This happened just before I ran away. It was the last act."

Zara sat patiently listening.

◆◆◆

Chapter 17

Joom's Guilty Secret

Joom gave a little cough, scratched behind his ear, and then began.

"Well," he said, his eyes looking at something in the distance. "Mr G was as ugly as ugly could be, not because his features were bad but because everyone could see the evil and barbarity on his face."

"What's barbarity?"

"It means extreme cruelty. I learnt that word from my old master," explained Joom. "He used to say some humans are worse than animals; they have a barbaric nature. Master Abu Moosa was the opposite of barbaric." He smiled when he spoke of his old master, and Zara could see how much he had loved him. "Mr G, on the contrary, was a cruel and savage beast. Obviously, no one was willing to marry him. He was rejected by every single girl even though he was immensely wealthy. No father would consider his hand in marriage for his daughter. They all turned him down with some excuse or the other."

"And with good reason too," said Zara.

"Then one day," went on Joom, "when G was hunting in the forest, he saw a most beautiful maiden by the river. She was singing a song to the birds and the trees and nature. She had a beautiful voice too.

"Of course, he went up to her and greeted her respectfully. He lied to her, telling her his name was Zola, pretending to be gentle and noble. He removed all the rich and gaudy rings from his fingers, and wore only a black onyx ring. He knew this girl would be turned off by gaudy

fashion and jewellery. He began visiting her every day without his hunting party, pretending to be tender-hearted, and paying her many compliments.

"She began believing him. He was very happy. At last, he'd get a wife. And such a beautiful and virtuous wife too. She had long black hair that fell below her waist, and her eyes were the deepest pools of black with stars shining from within them. So, as time went on, he proposed to her.

"She didn't accept immediately, but told him to give her some time. Some days later, while walking in the forest, she saw a deer struggling in a snare. It was a beautiful deer, with long antlers and an exquisite velvet coat. She rushed to help free her from the trap. 'Who has done this, you poor thing?' she cried, when she saw the cruel nails that had pierced the deer's long, slim legs. 'What a horrible snare this is.' "

"How could she speak to animals?" Zara asked.

"Oh, she was a child of the forest, so she knew the language of not just birds and animals but of every plant and every tree."

"Go on, Joom," said Zara. "What did the deer say?"

"'This is how that cruel hunter kills us,' the deer replied. She was now freed from the snare but was in tremendous pain. 'It's not a quick death. He likes to make us die slowly because he says the meat tastes better'."

"'Who is this hunter?' the girl asked.

"The deer described him, his cruel face with the long, black drooping moustache, and his eyes like thin slits. 'Sometimes, he pretends he's some tender and gentle man who wouldn't harm a fly,' said the deer.

"Now, something about this description sounded familiar. She realised with a start that it was the same gentle man who had asked for her hand in marriage. 'Does he wear a black onyx ring on his finger?' she asked the deer.

"'That's the man,' said the deer. 'The very same one.'

"Well, you can imagine what happened next. She was a maiden of the forests, so was not afraid of him. And she was angry at his cruelty, angry with herself for not seeing through him. So, when he came the next time, after having put a drop of oil in both his eyes to make himself appear teary, he got a very different reception. She flatly refused his proposal and told him to keep away from her.

"'Be off with you,' cried the beautiful maiden. 'You are known in these areas as a man of cruelty and brutality. I know how you kill the poor animals you hunt. I know how you treat your servants. I never want to see your face again.'

"She turned and walked away. The speech he'd prepared, the bouquet of red roses he'd bought her along with a pearl and ruby ring—all came to naught. He left the forest in a huff, along with his hunters, who were waiting a little further away. A rabbit wandered into his path, and he shot an arrow into her heart, leaving her quivering and half- dead. He kicked his dogs and his servants. He was in such a foul temper.

"And as soon as he returned to his dark

mansion, he summoned me. He told me what I should do." Here, Joom stopped, and took a big gulp.

Zara waited for him to continue, but the words seemed to be stuck within his throat. "Joom," she said gently, "you can tell me. I won't judge you, I promise."

Joom took another deep breath and then, as if forcing himself to go on, he continued, "This was the most evil act. He said I should go to the forest and throw a powder on the maiden, so that her face and body would spring out in ugly, painful sores that would never heal. She would be so unsightly that no one would marry her. If he couldn't have her, no one else could."

Zara shuddered, just thinking of the fate of the poor girl. "Joom, did you actually do such a wicked deed?"

Two little tears trickled down Joom's face, and fell with a plop on the balcony floor. "I'm a genie, little girl, remember? I have to obey my master. If he tells me to jump into a well, I have to do it. I can't disobey him."

Too late, Zara realised how much her words must have hurt him. "Oh, Joom, I'm sorry. I didn't mean to make you feel guilty. Of course, you have to do what is asked by your master. Don't feel bad, Joom. It's not your fault."

Joom shook his head. "No, it was my fault. I could have run away, like I did later. But I just didn't think I had any freedom of choice." He shook his head sadly. "He gave me a black pouch full of an evil powder that he had prepared using all kinds of poisonous things. He told me to climb up a tree and as soon as she came under it, to scatter it on her. He knew I'd never be visible, and she'd never look up. She used to sing to herself and walk along, so it was easy to find her. And she took the same path every day. He was hidden somewhere nearby to watch the fun.

"Oh, how loath I was to harm such a beautiful

and innocent girl who had stood up for herself. I took the pouch from him and set out. But I thought to myself, *let me at least throw in some pretty flowers that would fall on her before she was marred forever.* I did so, throwing in some roses and peonies and sweet-smelling jasmine into the black pouch.

"Well, as soon as I saw her, singing so beautifully, so one with nature, I just couldn't bring myself to open the pouch and release the powder. But I had to. So, without looking, I closed my eyes and I emptied the powder on her head when she was directly beneath me.

"I expected to hear her shrieking and screaming, but instead, I heard laughter. I opened my eyes, thinking she had become mad with grief at her fate. And what a surprise I got. Wherever she walked, flowers fell behind her, an entire carpet of flowers. Soon, the forest people and animals all came out and began bowing before her, calling her 'Queen of the Forest'.

"That evil man, hiding behind some giant trees, was shocked to see his powder hadn't worked. I pretended to know nothing about it, and didn't tell him I'd thrown in some flowers into the pouch. Evidently, those flowers had worked in some magical way on the powder, changing something horrible into something pure and beautiful. How happy I was that the evil powder was ineffective.

"Well, that black-hearted man could easily make out I was happy and thought I had something to do with it. He yelled at me, 'You useless piece of blubbering flesh. There's nothing you can do right, and you call yourself a genie! Come on here, you are going back into this stone urn and I'm going to throw you into the deepest ocean so you'll never be found ever again.'

"When he said these words, I fled. I was a young genie then, and could not just run but even fly, and very fast too. He obviously couldn't catch me. And his last words to me were, 'Wait till I catch you, you bumbling oaf. Even if it takes a thousand years, I'll hunt you out.'

"And that, my little human, is my own guilty story. I've lost even the little magic I once possessed. And I know Gorgonzola is hunting for me still."

Zara was quiet for a few moments after hearing this story. Poor Joom. How sad and guilty he felt. And it was no fault of his too.

"No, Joom, you're neither bad nor useless," said Zara. "Maybe you made a mistake, but how were you to know? After all, genies have to obey. And you never harmed that girl but saved her. That was so clever of you, to throw in flowers. Stop feeling so guilty, Joom."

"Do you really think so, that I'm not so bad?" Joom asked. "Cross your heart, little human. Don't say things just to please me. Tell me the truth."

Zara nodded solemnly. "Joom, you're certainly not bad, but have the kindest of hearts.

You have a very special gift, too, of making people feel better."

Joom smiled happily. "Is that so? Thank you, little human. In fact, you are the one who makes me feel good about myself. You're a real friend."

Zara smiled and hugged him. "I can go to bed dreaming of beautiful flowers. Goodnight." And she gave him a big kiss on his cheek, the cheek with a million, trillion wrinkles.

"Good night, little Zara. You've made my day. I didn't realise guilt could make my heart so heavy. Now, it feels so light and happy." He stood taller, straighter, and more confident. "Sweet dreams, dear human child."

And with those last words, Joom loped back into his tree-home, the tamarind tree with the long pods and bushy leaves.

◆◆◆

Chapter 18

Preparing for the Quiz

Dad's last day at school was drawing nearer. And so was the quiz date. Zara had set her heart on winning. So much depended on them getting the cup for the school (and maybe getting Mr Boyle and the board to change their minds?) and (fingers crossed), her winning that two lakh prize. The sponsors were international companies, so the prize was very high.

She was glad there was something for her to do to take her mind off her other problems. She and Ramu had to work at this together. The next day, as soon as school got over, she stood outside Ramu's class, watching the children stream out, carrying heavy bags and satchels on their shoulders. When Mr Dimpleby was headmaster, their bags were light. Not anymore. Her brown khaki satchel felt at least ten kilos heavier, although she knew it must be just a kilo more at the most.

She soon saw Ramu exit the room, his skinny shoulders stooped under the weight of his bag.

"Hey, Ramu. You carrying bricks or something?"

Ramu grinned. "Seems like it. But I can't blame the Boiled Egg. I'm carrying a few science quiz books that Mr Solomon gave me today."

"That's just what I've come to speak to you about," said Zara, removing her heavy bag from her shoulders to give herself a little rest. "Mr Solomon gave me some books too. I've left them at home. I think it's best if we prepare together. How about during the long lunch break? We can finish our lunch in ten minutes and then we'll have fifty minutes to prepare. That should be enough."

"Great idea," answered Ramu. "But where? It's so noisy then, with everyone on full lung-power."

Zara smiled. "How about in the library? No one comes there." She'd thought everything out the night before. This was her last chance. They *had* to win!

"Okay. Library it is. There's just a little over a week left for us to prepare. Are you all set?"

"Kind of," said Zara, hoisting her satchel once more over her shoulders. "But it's better to prepare together, so we're sure. See you tomorrow then."

Miss Ray, the librarian, who always had her nose in a book, looked up in surprise from what she was reading when the two students entered. She had a round face and wore thick, black-framed glasses that gave her an intellectual look. She and Zara got on very well, especially as she knew Dr Sameer well too.

"Well, well," said Miss Ray, "this is the very first time students are coming to the library during recess to study." She closed the book she was reading. Zara saw the title, 'Great Expectations' by Charles Dickens.

"We're preparing for the science quiz, miss," said Ramu. "Can we bring these books in? Mr Solomon gave them to us."

Miss Ray beamed. "Oh, in that case, take that study table in the far corner. But there should not be too much noise. I'll be sitting here reading, and I don't want any disturbance."

Zara and Ramu took a seat and brought out their books. Zara's topic was 'Adaptation of Animals and Plants', while Ramu's was 'Reptiles'. They exchanged books and began shooting questions at each other, making every attempt to keep their voices low.

"OK, answer this," said Ramu. "A camel is adapted to survive in desert conditions. Which of the following is NOT true?

(a) The hump is used to store fat.

(b) The nostrils can close to keep sand out.

(c) They have large feet so they do not sink in soft sand.

(d) They have long eyelashes to attract other camels."

Zara laughed. "It's d," she said. "These are real camels, not cartoon camels. OK, my turn. Which reptile's tongue is twice the length of its body? It is:

(a) Gecko

(b) Chameleon

(c) Anaconda

(d) Frog."

"The answer's b, chameleon," said Ramu. "Their tongues are twice the size of their bodies. Imagine that in a human!"

"That'd be ten to twelve feet long," said Zara.

"How did you get this great idea?" Ramu asked after they'd quizzed each other for over half an hour. "It's so much easier and more fun to prepare together."

Zara beamed. "I hope we win the cup this time."

"By the way," said Ramu, "where are those

pals of yours? The two who hang out with you?"

"Oh, Mimi and Pixie? They're around somewhere." Zara had never been separated from her friends. The trio were always together. "I do miss roaming around with them," she said. Then a new idea hit her. "Hey, Ramu, would you mind if my friends join us? They can ask us the questions. It'll be more fun".

"Fine with me," said Ramu.

"OK, I'll ask them today."

But Mimi and Pixie didn't seem very keen.

"We do miss you, Zara," said Mimi. "But Ramu? He's strange. He doesn't seem to have any friends in his class."

"Yes, look how he hunches and walks around alone, smiling to himself. He's so stuck up," added Pixie.

Zara was quick in his defence. "Not at all. He likes being alone, and it's not that he has no friends. The children in his class really like him. He helps them all and even explains hard stuff to them. He just likes being alone during recess. He said he thinks over stuff."

"I heard his dad's a scientist and his mom's a computer expert," said Mimi, still not convinced. "Like, she helps prevent hacking. A very brainy job."

"Look, why don't you two come tomorrow during the recess and see for yourselves?" Zara said. "He's really very nice and helpful."

"Yes, but I heard he's a nerd. He reads the encyclopaedia in the toilet." Both Pixie and Mimi giggled.

The three of them had seen how Ramu'd been teased when he joined the school a couple of years ago because he wasn't tall and brawny but had a big head. The boys in his class nicknamed him 'Bighead on the Block'.

"Please, you two," said Zara, looking at Pixie and Mimi through her thick glasses. "Just give him a chance. We have all the questions ready for you to ask."

"We quiz you two?" Pixie asked. "Oh, what

fun. I didn't know that's what you wanted from us."

"Of course, we'll do it," said Mimi, giving Zara a hug. "We want you to win."

Miss Ray was taken aback when she saw the four enter together. Zara noticed she had read almost to the end of her book, which she closed after bookmarking the page.

"Oh my! What have we here? A quartet. Are you both also taking part in the science quiz?" she asked. "I know only two representatives are chosen from each school."

"No, Miss,' said Mimi. "But we've come to help them out by asking them questions from the quiz books. We want our school to get back the cup."

Miss Ray yawned. Her eyes were on her book. "If I hear any loud chatter, all four of you will have to leave," she said.

"But we can talk a little, can't we Miss? They'll be asking us questions and we'll be answering.

Like in an actual quiz." Zara wanted to be safe.

"That's fine," said Miss Ray, looking impatiently at her book. "Now, just remember what I said."

The four children seated themselves at the far end. It was a big library with books and computers and plenty of tables and chairs. Zara and Ramu handed over the quiz books and Mimi and Pixie took turns to ask questions. It was like a real quiz.

"It's fun to be a quizmaster," said Mimi. "Like I can pretend to be cleverer than what I am as if I know all the answers."

Pixie nodded. "You two are doing great. How do you know the answers so well?"

"We're not so great," said Ramu modestly. "We're interested in the science subjects. I'm sure I won't be as good as you in your favourite subjects."

"Pixie's the best in English," said Zara. "She

has such a big vocabulary, and is Miss D'Souza's favourite. And Mimi is Mrs Abraham's favourite because she's so good in history."

"How do you remember all those dates?" Ramu asked.

"C'mon, nerd. You can remember every single date," said Mimi, giving Ramu a playful punch. "You walked away with every subject prize last year."

The two girls began to warm up to him. He had a good sense of humour too. He made the girls double up in laughter with some of his descriptions of the teachers. Especially of Mr Boyle who nobody liked.

"Yesterday, Rohan got boiled eggs to school. And when Mr Boyle passed by, he took an egg out and pretended to eat it."

They all laughed, a little too loudly, and Miss Ray looked up from her book.

"Sorry, Miss," said Ramu, before she could say anything more.

The training was tough but fun, especially with Mimi and Pixie joining in. Mr Solomon once popped into the library during recess, and saw the four of them busy.

"I hope they're not troubling you, Miss Ray," he said.

"Not at all," she answered. "I wish we had more students like them."

The preparation didn't just end with books. Ramu and Zara watched many DVDs too after school hours. It was hard for Zara, with her failing eyesight, to watch the educational videos on the home computer, but she managed, her eyes scrunched up, notebook in hand, taking down points.

"You poor child! How late are you going to stay up? How pale and weak you've become," said Mom, when she found Zara watching a programme late at night a couple of days before the quiz.

"Mom, it's fine. I don't mind staying up late. I just want to win that cup for our school." She wanted to add, 'also two lakh rupees'.

Zara's eyes gleamed behind her thick glasses when she thought of the money. In her own small way, she could contribute to the operation. Plus, it was such a prestige to win that cup—a huge silver cup with all the famous scientists' names engraved on it. It was a rotating cup, which meant that the school that won that year got to keep it until the next year.

Delhi International School had won the last three years, and Mr Solomon was very keen that Summerdale High win back the cup. Zara overheard her father telling her mother that Mr Boyle was putting a lot of pressure on poor Mr Solomon, threatening him with a pay cut or, even worse, of losing his job if they didn't win.

"You two have to be the saviours of Summerdale High School," he told them. "Your names will be put up on the board as the winners, all emblazoned in gold, and your pictures will appear in the newspapers as well as in our school magazine. Imagine that!"

In these ways, Mr Solomon both goaded and encouraged them.

"Gosh, Sir seems more stressed than us," said Ramu. "What if we don't win? Last year, it seems he told the two participants exactly what your mother told you, to work hard and enjoy the quiz."

"Last year, it was Mr Dimpleby who was the headmaster," said Mimi. "Now, it's Mr Boyle."

"That explains it," said Pixie, and the others agreed.

"School has become so hard," said Zara, pulling a long face.

"Mr Dimpleby was so relaxed about things," said Ramu. "Even the teachers were happier. Now, they all look sad and angry."

Zara thought of the piles of books her mother brought home to correct every day, staying up late at night to finish. And as for Dad—the number of times he'd stayed back after school hours to finish work. And still, he'd lost his job.

Zara knew Mom and Dad tried hard to make things as normal as possible for her, but she couldn't help but notice their drawn faces. Dad was a slim man of medium height, but now, he actually looked skinny. He had a big nose with a knob in the middle, and that bony bit became more pronounced as the days went by.

He spent all his spare time applying for different jobs or taking online tuitions. Mom no longer cooked delicious food like she used to do earlier. Zara didn't complain. But she missed eating pancakes for breakfast, and spicy stews and yummy muffins. Mom was an excellent cook, and Dad and Zara helped her whenever they could. Not anymore.

Some nights before the quiz, Zara was working in her room at night after her parents had gone to bed. They didn't know she was awake and reading a quiz book by the light of her bedroom lamp. Then she heard Dad tell Mom something, and Mom saying, "Oh no!"

She strained hard to hear, and distinctly heard Dad telling her to shush. "I don't want Zara to know this," he said. So, it concerned her. She didn't mean to eavesdrop, but she went close to the wall to hear what they were saying. But it was no use. Their voices were low, too low.

The next morning, they looked even sadder, if that were possible at all. "Mom, Dad, what happened? Tell me," said Zara.

"Nothing's happened, child," said Mom. "How's your science quiz preparation? I saw that you were working till late at night. And did you enjoy the video Mr Solomon told you to watch?"

"Yes, Mom," said Zara. "It was about atoms and molecules. I hope we win the cup and bring the school some glory."

Mom and Dad remained strangely quiet at this statement. They would normally have encouraged her, but this time, they looked at each other sadly.

Dad spoke up. "Zara, please remember, it's just a quiz competition. Somebody has to win and somebody has to lose. And if you lose, it really doesn't matter. Last year and the year before too, Summerdale never won."

But Zara was all set on winning. "Dad, my name and picture will come in the local papers! That'll be so exciting." She didn't mention the two lakh rupees if she won the prize for best overall participant, as her parents discouraged her from talking of money. And a tiny voice within her said that perhaps, just perhaps, Mr Boyle and the board would change their minds about dismissing Dad when they saw how much prestige she brought to the school. She and Ramu had to win!

Mom cut in, "Zara, it's good to be ambitious and have dreams. But also be realistic. Otherwise, you'll set yourself up for a big disappointment."

Mom always had the last word.

◆◆◆

Chapter 19

Joom Gets Bolder

Zara continued with her quiz preparation, but also met Joom every night. She was careful not to sleep too late, and Joom, like a good elder, reminded her to return at midnight.

"I feel like Cinderella," giggled Zara. "The clock strikes twelve, and I have to return. Back to bed."

"Well, human Zara, you need at least seven hours of sleep. Right now, you're getting only six."

"How long do you sleep, Joom?" Zara asked, getting up to quietly return to her room. "You can sleep the whole day if you want."

"No, little human, genies don't need much sleep. But I'm doing lots of things in the tree. Like I clean the branches and help the mother birds when the babies are naughty."

"Oh, how do you do that?" Zara asked in surprise.

"Well, when one of the chicks is greedy or fights with its brothers and sisters all that the mother bird has to say is, 'Wait, I'll call Uncle Joom.'"

"And do they then start behaving?"

Joom grinned. "Not any more, little human. When she says she'll call Uncle Joom, they say, 'Yes, please call Uncle Joom. We want to have a bit of fun. We love jumping on his big stomach.'"

Zara laughed. Whenever she was with Joom, she forgot all her problems. But suddenly she remembered something that had been worrying her. "Joom, I know something has happened, but Dad and Mom aren't telling me."

"Well, maybe it'll trouble your mind and you

have to concentrate on this quiz preparation. Maybe that's why they aren't telling you," said Joom. "Your parents care for you very much."

"Of course they do," said Zara. "But that doesn't mean they can't tell me. I mean, I know how much this operation costs and that Dad's lost his job, and that horrid Adam Butt and his father have complained about him. Even about Mr Boyle, our headmaster—they now talk about him openly in front of me. We all loved and respected Mr Dimpleby, but Mr Boyle—everyone is just scared of him."

"He sounds just like Gorgonzola, my evil master," said Joom. "Outwardly jolly, but inwardly cruel and evil."

"Joom, you're saying his name! Gorgonzola! He's just a smelly old cheese."

"Gorgonzola," repeated Joom. "I'm no longer afraid of him. And that's because of you, little Zara, telling me not to feel guilty, telling me how brave I am. I can now shout out his name."

Joom leaned across the balcony, cupped both his hands around his mouth and was about to yell out the name when Zara pulled on his arm with a loud *shhh*.

"Are you mad?" she asked. "Mom and Dad, in fact the whole neighbourhood will hear you."

Joom put a big hand over his mouth. "*Oops*, I forgot," he said. "Sorry, little one, you were talking about something so serious. Please go on."

"When I told them I was hoping we'd win the cup for the school, they weren't very encouraging," continued Zara. "I wonder why, Joom. It'll be super if we won."

"Yes, and you can eat so much ice-cream from that silver cup," said Joom.

Zara laughed. "Joom, you're so, so funny. That silver cup will be displayed in school. We won't get to take it home. But I do so want to win the prize money. Imagine, two whole lakhs! It'll help Mom and Dad so much."

"Two lakh pieces of gold must be so heavy,"

said Joom. "A whole sack, maybe two whole sacks! Little Zara, if you win that grand prize, I'll carry it all the way for you to Boss Danglies."

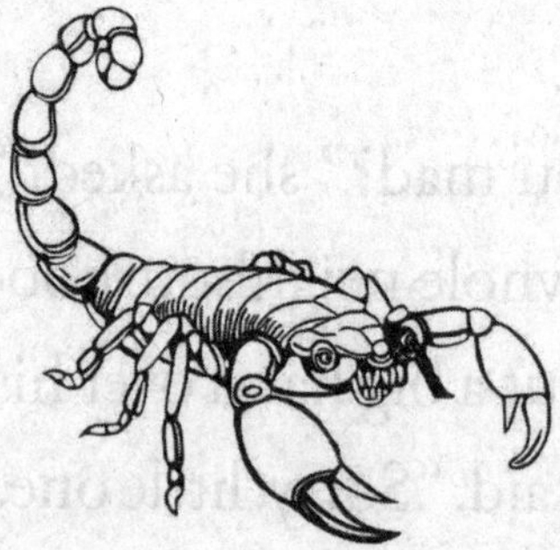

Zara smiled, not trying to explain to Joom that paper money was quite different. She wished him a good night, and quietly went back to her room. Neither of them noticed the black scorpion that had crept inside the balcony and hiding in a corner, watching silently, and once again scuttling away into the night.

◆◆◆

Chapter 20

The Night Before the Quiz

It was the night before the quiz. Zara went to bed early, but sleep would not come. She could hear her parents talking in low tones, and then that too stopped. The hours ticked by. She'd told Joom the previous night that she wouldn't be meeting him the next day.

"You need all the rest you can get, little one," Joom had said. "My old master, Abu Moosa, always used to say early to bed, early to rise, makes a man live a full life."

She tossed and turned in her bed. She closed her eyes tight and tried counting sheep, like she was taught to do. But, no sleep. Finally, she sat up and turned towards her window.

"Let me see what Joom's up to," she said. She heard Dad's steady snores and Mom's regular breathing. It was past midnight. She quietly let herself out into the balcony. Joom was sprawled out, juggling three round pebbles and catching them deftly.

"I thought I shouldn't disturb you today," he said. "Tomorrow's your quiz."

"I just can't seem to get any sleep," said Zara, taking her usual position opposite him, her feet stretched out on the balcony floor. "Joom, can you tell me another story? Tell me how you left your old master and got picked up by Gorgonzola?"

"That's a long story," said Joom. "But I'll try to tell it as briefly as I can." He settled himself more comfortably against the wall, sprawling out over almost the entire balcony.

"Well, the city of Petra where I lived was built of red sandstone. It was a beautiful city, with walkways and arches and a very good drainage system. All the waste water would flow out of the houses and into an underground pond where it would be filtered by sparkling gemstones before it came up again in springs.

"Me and some of my genie friends used to have so much fun sliding down the drains, romping around in the underground pond, and then emerging from the springs in the mountains. Then we'd make the return journey. We used to have so many fun competitions, seeing who'd come first.

"Well, one day, when we were up to our usual mischief in the drains, we felt a huge shudder. Then suddenly, the earth opened up into deep valleys. 'What's happening?' we yelled out. But the earth began folding and shaking even more, and we screamed in terror. We were all young genies and didn't know any powerful spells that would pull us out. Then, to my shock, all my friends disappeared into the folds. I was at the edge of a deep crevice. I looked down and it was bottomless. And the edge was slippery with ice."

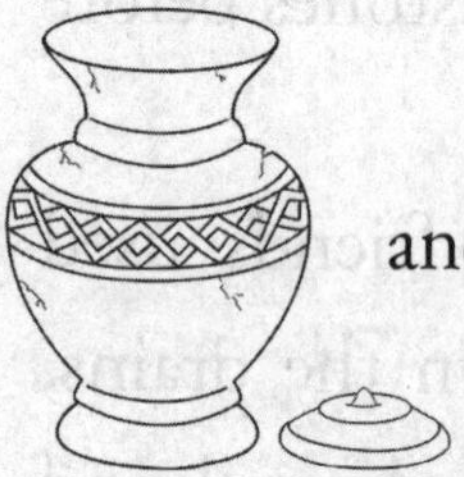

"Oh no, Joom, did you fall down?"

Joom nodded. "I lost my foothold and fell and fell, maybe millions of miles—at least, that's what it felt like. Then, when I came to my senses, I saw that I was again shut up in an old stone urn. I lay there, sleeping for many hundreds of years, when I was suddenly woken up by a loud, barking sound.

"I shot out of the urn and bowed low before my new master. I honestly thought it would be a ferocious dog, but it was a vile-looking human with glittering eyes and a long, droopy moustache over pointy, misshapen teeth. When he saw me pop out of the stone urn, he gave a crooked smile. My heart missed a beat because I knew instinctively he would be a cruel master.

"'Oho, a genie,' he said, and cracked his whip. 'I am in need of a genie.' I bowed again. 'Boy, do you know mageek?' He said 'mageek,' not 'magic.' He had a funny way of speaking.

"'Yes, my master,' I stammered. 'I am not very good in magic spells, but I can do a little magic.' I didn't tell him that very few of my spells worked, and most of the time, I bungled things up.

" 'Veerrrryyy goood,' he said. He was dragging out his e's and o's and rolling his r's. 'I will trrrain youuu to dooo my bidding.'

"Then he cracked his whip again, and yelled at me in a terrible voice, 'This meeans get back into yourrr urn, youuu foool.' I jumped back inside, shuddering in fear, wondering where I had landed up."

"Were you still in Petra?"

"I was in the desert near Petra, in no-man's land. He called himself Gorgonzola, and told everyone that he was a rich merchant. But he was actually a robber who used to wander around, stealing and killing and pillaging. The tribes who lived in the desert dreaded him and did not allow him to live with them. They knew he was nothing but trouble, and quietly gave him whatever he wanted, gold and silver and food and other bounties, and bade him go from their camp.

"They knew he would take stuff by force so they preferred pleasing him and sending him on his way. Not that he wanted to be part of any tribe. He was a loner, and liked to roam the wilds on his camel with a lean and ferocious wolf by his side."

Zara's eyes became round with fear. "It's good you ran away from him," she said.

"Well, so far I've escaped him," said Joom, "but who knows when he'll catch me?" His big, chubby shoulders shook with fear.

"He won't catch you. This tamarind tree has so many leaves and branches, and those long pods make good sticks for defending yourself. Nobody can find you here."

"I do hope so," said Joom, giving a frightened look behind him. Then, gathering himself up, he said, "OK, now, little one, time to go to bed. Tomorrow's an important day for you. Good night." And he gave Zara a big hug.

Unknown to the two of them, a coal-black bat was hanging upside-down from one of the branches of the tamarind tree. In the darkness, it looked like a huge pod. But its eyes were wide open, and it was listening to their conversation with great interest and curiosity. When it saw it had ended, the bat flew into the dark night, its huge, webbed wings flapping silently.

◆◆◆

Chapter 21

D-day Arrives

The students in the giant auditorium in Delhi International School were silent. It was the most prestigious quiz for junior school students, this inter-school science quiz. Forty-five schools from seven major cities had participated, and now only four schools qualified for the final round.

The quiz master, Mr Davin Dey, (who jokingly called himself D-Dey), had been specially flown in, courtesy the Association of Schools and Educational Institutions, just for this occasion. He was well-known to the schools as he had been the chief quizmaster for many years. A small, dapper man, he had something of an entertainer about him with his bright jackets and spiky hair.

Today, he'd worn a black jacket with silver sequins glittering all over, like a magician's costume. But no matter how strangely he dressed, he brought a smile to everyone's face with his antics and gentle teasing. He knew how to put the participants at ease as well as make the audience laugh with his funny and clever jokes.

The four teams that were participating—Delhi International School (the hosts), The International Academy of Scholars, Greyfriars Academy and Summerdale High School—were seated on stage, and giant screens were put up around the auditorium so that all the participants were visible.

So far, the hosts, DIS, and Summerdale High School, were leading. But the other two schools were not far behind. It was the 'lucky dip' round.

Ramu and Zara sat erect and unmoving, their fingers on the electronic buzzer. The two often exchanged glances.

It's good we get on well, thought Zara. *And though he's a year senior to me, he never bosses over me.*

The auditorium, with a seating capacity for five hundred, was packed. The junior school students of DIS were seated at the back, along with students from various other schools. Each school could send fifteen students as 'cheerleaders' to encourage their team. Zara knew that Mimi and Pixie were seated there somewhere.

She scanned the auditorium, and saw the red blazers of Summerdale High. And there—both her friends were waving at her. She was too shy to wave back, and wondered if they'd be able to make out she was smiling at them. Right in the front row were the two people who were the most important in her life: Mom and Dad. Fortunately, the quiz was on a Saturday, a holiday.

At first, Dad had refused to come, but Mom had insisted. "It's for Zara's sake," she said. "This is such an important occasion and parents have been specially invited. We just HAVE to go to cheer Zara and Ramu."

Zara didn't blame Dad for not wanting to come. He was leaving school after a week, and as that dreadful day was fast approaching, he'd sunk into a depression. She was so grateful that he had come, just for her sake.

Zara caught both their eyes, and Mom gave a thumbs-up sign. Since they were seated right in front of the stage, Zara could see them quite clearly. Dad gave her a very tiny smile. She loved the way Dad smiled. It was not a big smile like Mom's, but his eyes crinkled at the corners and his mouth just went up a little. This was enough for her. She was charged, and she vowed to do her best.

Now, it was the deciding round. The entire auditorium was quiet. The air was thick with anticipation. But Mr D Dey paused, as someone important had just entered the auditorium. Zara watched as the headmaster of Delhi International School led that person to the front seat. Her heart sank. The figure was familiar. It was Mr Boyle, making a grand entrance. Ramu nudged Zara.

"The Boiled Egg's arrived," he said, and Zara giggled. She stole a look at her parents, and saw her father sit back in his seat, as if hiding, after seeing Mr Boyle.

"Dad," she said in her mind, "wait and see. I'll make you proud."

"So now," said Mr D Dey, "we have the deciding round. It's a lucky dip, so each team gets to pick a number, and the question for that number will be put up on the screen. Is that clear to all?"

The eight participants nodded. Mr D Dey danced up to the first team, proffering a straw basket with numbered tiles inside."Okay, one of you stick your appendage into this basket and pick out a number." He winked at the audience. "These are all our future scientists, so they'll know the meaning of appendage. When I was their age, I always thought it was a kind of bandage." The audience laughed.

DIS picked out a number. It was 7. The question appeared on the big screen. Mr D Dey read it out.

"Which of the following metals is a liquid at room temperature?

(a) Lithium
(b) Magnesium
(c) Mercury, or
(d) Sodium."

Both students pressed the buzzer, but one had pressed it a little earlier.

"It's C, mercury."

"That is correct. Five points to DIS. The score now stands: DIS 540, Summerdale High at 535, Greyfriarsis is at 530, and the International Academy of Scholars is also at 530. Now, let's go on to Greyfriars School. Ah, they've chosen number 13. Lucky for some, number 13. Let's see what the question is. Which energy emerges from motion?

(a) Potential energy
(b) Electrical energy
(c) Gravitational energy, or
(d) Kinetic energy"

The two-boy team of Greyfriars both shouted out, "D. Kinetic energy."

"Please, boys, we can't have you shouting like this. Only one of you has to give the answer. Is that clear?"

The two looked a little sheepish and nodded.

"Anyway," went on Mr D Dey, "kinetic energy or D is the correct answer. So, fivc points to Greyfriars, which brings their total to 535.

"Ok, now on to the International Academy of Scholars. Now, let's see what's in store for them. Ah, two fat majors, 88. How many of you adults in this audience play Bingo?"

Many hands went up. "Happy to see I'm not

out of place among these youngsters here," said Mr D Dey, beaming. "Ok, now, let's see what the majors have in store for you. Here's the question. Which biologist proposed the theory of evolution through natural selection?

(a) Charles Darwin

(b) Stephen Hawking

(c) Francesco Redi, or

(d) Alexander Fleming ."

There was a big buzz of excitement through the audience because just about everybody knew the answer to this easy question.

"It's A, sir, Charles Darwin." This was answered by the first buzzer, a girl with an unruly mop of curly hair that kept getting into her eyes.

"Are you sure?" Mr D Dey asked.

The girl nodded, her curls dancing over her face.

"Are you sure you're sure?"

"Yes, I am."

"Yes, you are right. It's Charles Darwin. So,

their score also goes up 5 points to 535. Now, for Summerdale."

He took the little basket to Zara and Ramu.

"You pick," whispered Ramu to her.

Zara put her hand into the basket, praying that it would be an easy one, or else DIS would win. She picked out number 10.

"Ah, you've got Downing Street there," smiled Mr D Dey. The question flashed on the screen while he read it out.

"Blood is made up of how many parts?

(a) 5 (b) 4

(c) 3 (d) 6"

Zara and Ramu looked at each other, delighted at such an easy question. "You answer," whispered Zara.

Ramu pressed the buzzer, and gave the answer, "It's B or 4."

"And can one of you, Ramu or Zara, name the four parts?"

That was easy. Only three nights earlier, Zara had watched a science show about the constitution of blood. "It's plasma, red blood cells, white blood cells and platelets," answered Zara.

"Now, you are one smart cookie," said Mr D Dey, admiration writ on his face. "Four it is, or B. I wish I could give you extra points for naming them too. But that was just an extra question. So, Summerdale High School also gets five points, which brings their total score to 540."

The big screen showed the latest marks.

DIS: 540

Summerdale: 540

Greyfriars: 535

International Academy of Scholars: 535.

"Uh-oh," said Mr D Dey. "We have a problem here. There's a tie between Summerdale and the hosts, DIS. And we can't divide the cup into half, now, can we?"

"No," screamed out all the children. And then a chant was taken up, "DIS, DIS, DIS, DIS."

"What about Summerdale then?" Mr D Dey joked. "I can see that they are greatly outnumbered in the audience by the host school. OK, I have a solution. I'll ask the last question. It's worth fifty points, and is open to all four teams. Whoever gets to the buzzer first gets to answer. And if they get it wrong, it goes to the person who was second on the buzzer. It's all computerised up to the last nanosecond, so there can be no favouring. Is it ok for all?"

"Yes," shouted out all the children.

The last question. It was a matter of winning or losing. All four teams sat up straight, their hands on the buzzer. One of them, the girl with curly hair from International Academy of Scholars, pressed it by mistake, and it rang loud and long.

"Oops, sorry," she said.

"It's just nerves," said Mr D Dey, smiling. "I'm sure everybody's hearts are palpitating. This is the clincher, and worth 50 points. So, all four teams have an equal chance of winning the cup. Are you all ready?" he asked, turning towards the teams. They did not answer, but looked at him, nervous smiles on their faces, one hand extended and touching the buzzer.

Zara noticed that she was the only left-handed one. All the others had their right hands out. She scolded herself for noticing such a silly little detail. *Focus on the question, girl*, she warned herself, *and get to that buzzer first.*

"OK," said Mr D Dey, "listen to this question carefully. It has only one correct answer. Ready? Scientists believe that the continents of the earth were all one large landmass 280 million years ago. The moving of tectonic plates caused this mass to break off into different pieces, making up the continents as we know them today. What was this landmass called?"

Zara knew the answer. So did the others. The ringers screamed, and the numbers came up on the screen. Zara stared. Her number was second. The DIS boy had been first on the buzzer.

There was another hush, as Mr D Dey continued, "OK, Kabeer from DIS was first on the buzzer. Kabeer, if you don't get this right, it'll go to the next person, who is Zara from Summerdale."

While he was speaking, Zara stole a look at her parents. She had let them down! She'd let her school down. She could feel a little tear at the corner of her eye. Nobody could see it because of her glasses. All this hard work for nothing. She'd just go totally blind, and have to go to that special school.

A big black lump rose in her throat. She thought of Joom and all the encouraging and positive words he had told her. "Joom, it's all rubbish what you said," she told herself. Life stretched out, one grey and murky path, ahead of her. No blue skies, no rainbows.

The boy from DIS leaned back into his chair and spoke into the mike. "It's called 'continental drift'," he said with an air of great confidence.

Mr D Dey did not say anything. The audience was buzzing like a bee, and some of the DIS students were smiling and exchanging high-fives. They were sure they'd won.

"Continental drift, did you say? Are you sure?"

"Yes, I am," said the boy. "Hundred percent sure." He beamed, already appearing the champion.

Mr D Dey gave him a long, hard look. The DIS students were cheering and yelling, sure that they were once again going to get the cup. They waited for Mr D Dey to say, in his usual dramatic way when someone had won, that this was the right answer. He was purposely keeping quiet so that the tension would build up.

"I'm sorry, that's not the right answer."

There was a stunned silence, but Mr D Dey continued as if nothing had happened, "I am now going to ask Zara of Summerdale High School. Zara, what is your answer?"

The tension was so thick, that a knife would have cut through it. What would happen if Zara also got it wrong?

"Pangea," said Zara, without any hesitation.

"The land mass was called Pangea." She spelt it out. " P A N G E A."

Mr D Dey again was quiet. The audience too was silent. If Zara got it wrong, then it would go to the third team, and then the fourth. If all four got it wrong, there would probably be one more question, and then, if that too was inconclusive, the cup would go to the two schools that had equal marks, six months in one school and six months in the other. That would be the most disappointing win of all.

Mr D Dey looked at the audience and smiled. "And she's right," he said, before everybody jumped out of their seats, loudly clapping and cheering.

The Summerdale students were dancing in

their places, and began shouting out in chorus, "Summerdale, Summerdale, Summerdale."

The DIS students were good sports, and clapped and congratulated them. Zara was too shocked to say anything. Ramu formally shook hands with her, and whispered, "You've done it! You're a champ!"

"No, Ramu, we've done it, together, you and me."

◆◆◆

Chapter 22

After the Quiz

They'd won! Zara's dream had come true. How thrilled and happy Mom and Dad would be. She turned towards them, a big smile on her face, and saw them looking down. Mom took a tissue and wiped the corner of her eye. They were the opposite of happy. Perhaps they were crying out of sheer happiness?

Zara had read a quote that said something similar, that excess of sorrow, laughs and excess of joy, weeps. It was by a poet called William Blake who lived many centuries ago. It was a strange reaction. Especially for Dad. She then saw Mr Boyle approach, a fake smile stuck on his face.

The rest of the evening had the quality of an unreal but very pleasant dream. The headmaster of DIS, Mr Kapoor, gave a very encouraging speech to the winners, and to his disappointed school.

"Congratulations to all of you. We are very proud of all the participants, whether they won or not. It is also encouraging to know that so many of you are interested in the sciences. The questions were not easy, and I am glad to note that the teams tackled them with ease.

"But there can only be one winner, and Summerdale High School, represented by Zara of grade 6 and Ramu Damodar of grade 7, have clinched this year's title of 'Most Talented Students'. The cup goes to you. Your school, your headmaster, your teachers and your parents must be so proud of you. As we all are. Please come to accept the prize."

The two walked up to the podium, to

clapping so loud that their eardrums almost burst, and accepted the cup. Zara was openly crying, and stumbled while walking back.

"Ramu, we did it," she said. "We actually won."

But there was more to come.

"There's one more prize, a very generous cash prize of two lakhs given by Xcell Biotics, the main sponsor of this event, for the best student who answered the highest number of questions correctly. And that prize goes to—"

There was again silence. Who would get this huge sum of money? For them to keep?

"The computer cannot lie, and has tallied everyone's answers. And the one who got the most correct is—Zara Kumar of Summerdale."

Then Zara had to pose alone, holding up her cheque, and once again the flashlights almost blinded her. Ramu knew of her problem, and gently helped her to cross the stage and accept the cheque from the headmaster. There was more clapping and cheering.

Then, Mr Boyle came up on stage, and the

flashbulbs again went crazy. *Click, click, click*. Mr Boyle stood next to Zara, smiling as if he had won the prize. He stood in the middle, flanked by Zara and Ramu, and made a speech about how proud he was of them and how they'd brought back the reputation of the school.

Somehow, Zara found herself with her parents and with Mr Solomon after all the shouting and cheering had subsided. Ramu stood with his parents, looking happy and proud.

"I think both of you need to get back home and catch up on your sleep. But first of all, thank your teacher for all the hard work he personally has put in," Dad reminded her of what was important. "Know your priorities," he always said.

But before she could thank Mr Solomon, the large figure of Mr Boyle in his favourite black suit came up to them. "Well done," he said. "Ramu, we are very proud of you."

He patted Ramu on his back and left. Zara wondered why he hadn't said a word to her. Ramu whispered in her ear, "Don't take it to heart that the Boiled Egg didn't say anything to you. His head's scrambled." She felt so much better after hearing that. But then she saw her father, looking furious, and remembered Mr Boyle's unkind comment.

"Dad," she first hugged him and then her mother. "We won."

"We are so proud of you," they both said. But they still looked sad.

Then she heard Mr Solomon tell her father, "Boyle can't throw me out now."

"I don't know why he didn't call you up on stage, when you've done the maximum work to get this prize back to the school," said Dr Sameer.

The Summerdale students crowded around Zara and Ramu. "Hip, hip hurray! We've won," they shouted. "All thanks to Ramu and Zara."

There was more shouting and jollity. It was an unreal moment for Zara, this win. *Perhaps, just perhaps, Dad would be told to continue?*

"Can we have the winners doing a high-five?" A loud voice cut into her thoughts.

It was a reporter from the Daily Star. Ramu and Zara dutifully posed, holding the cup between them and doing a high-five with their free hands. Then, it seemed like a horde of reporters had descended on them, as flashbulbs once again exploded. Zara tried to make her eyes big behind her glasses, but each time, she had to close them as the lights flashed. Finally, they left.

It was while they were walking back to their car that Zara noticed a black shadow following her, but when she turned, it had disappeared.

◆◆◆

Chapter 23

Dreams to Dust

That night, Zara had the soundest sleep ever. Joom peeped in but decided not to knock on the window and wake her up. *She'll let me know what happened in the quiz tomorrow,* he thought.

The next morning, she was surprised to see Mom and Dad sitting at the dining table with backs straight and a grim expression on their faces. Today's breakfast was just plain boiled eggs and toast. She was a little disappointed. Mom could have made her a better, more celebratory breakfast. And Sunday breakfasts were always special. Mom sometimes made puris and spicy fried potatoes, and once had surprised her with waffles. *But this? Eggs and toast?*

They also didn't look happy or elated. Zara had given the cheque to Dad as soon as she had received it. He had hugged her close and said he was immensely proud of her. They'd all gone to Zara's favourite restaurant, Pizza Hut, for an early dinner. There was a special deal going on, two for the price of one.

Mom liked pizza with lots of vegetable toppings, but this time they let Zara choose; she chose margarita, although she *did* feel a little guilty that she was getting her way. Then she'd been treated to a huge ice-cream cone in her most-loved flavour, pistachio. It was a beautiful end to a beautiful day, and they'd all been so happy. But now?

"Zara, we have something important to tell you," said Mom after they'd cleared the table and washed the dishes.

"Sit here," said Dad. "I think I should be the one telling you."

Zara once again sat at the dining table with her parents seated opposite her. Dad cleared his throat, as if what he was going to say was something not very pleasant.

"You know that I have to leave the school within the next week. My job ends. This is my very last week. You know that, don't you?" Dad came straight to the point.

Zara nodded. Dad was fired. He'd been unfair to a boy. The whole school knew about it. But she was hoping that winning this cup and the best student prize would make the board and Mr Boyle change their minds. Besides, Mr Boyle had seen with his own eyes how she and Ramu had won back the cup for the school.

"Is it about the money for the operation? Dad, won't that cash prize I won help a little?"

"Of course it will, child," said Dad, giving a

desperate ‘how-can-I-say-this’ look to his wife. “And I’ll also take a bank loan. I told you I made a promise to take you to Los Angeles, and I’ll keep it.”

Zara’s eyes filled with tears. “Dad, you’ll have to work so hard to pay back that loan. And you too, Mom. I really wish we were rich! And why do I have to have this problem, of losing my eyesight? No one else in my class has this problem. Why only me? Why is life so unfair?”

Mom patted her on her shoulder. “Don’t worry, Zara. There are many ways of repaying the loan,” she said. “And there’s a solution for your eyes, isn’t there?”

Zara nodded.

Dad cleared his throat. “I have some other sad news to break to you. I have to tell you now, or else it’ll come as a bigger shock.”

What now? Zara turned to give him her full attention. Was that what they had been discussing behind closed doors, and out of her earshot?

"You can no longer attend this school. Your education so far was free. That was one of the perks I was getting. But since I've been told to go, unfortunately, Zara, you too will have to leave. I can't afford these school fees." Dad spoke as if he had rehearsed these lines. As if he had to say them.

Zara stared at him. She tried to say something, opened and shut her mouth, but no sound came, and her eyes behind the ugly glasses grew big.

"I have to leave my school and all my friends? And go to the special school?"

"I'm sorry, my child, I've failed you so much. Both of you." His face was a picture of misery, mouth drooping down, and (as Zara noticed with a start), his nails bitten to the quick. His hair had grown a little longer, and was balding in the middle of his head. Where was her smart, clever father, the father who was always encouraging and in control, who was so careful of his dress and deportment, and who carried himself with pride? He looked defeated.

"No!" Zara said, getting up from the table. "Dad, don't tell me I have to leave too?"

Dad nodded. "We can't afford paying these fees. This is the most expensive school in the city."

Zara turned to her mother, who was sitting with a sad expression, her face tight and pinched. "Mom, you're still a teacher in this school. Aren't you entitled to have a child studying free? Or can't you pay reduced fees?"

Mom swallowed, looked away, and then faced Zara. "I'm just a junior teacher. I'm not yet made permanent. So, I'm not entitled to these kind of perks. And if I pay the fees, even reduced fees, we'll have no money to eat."

Zara was ready to cry, but somehow the tears did not come. This was beyond tears. She put on a brave face. What was the point of making things worse by bursting into tears and running off to her room? No, she must have self-control. Leaving Summerdale High School where she'd been her whole life, right from kindergarten, leaving her dear friends and teachers behind—it was unthinkable. Even in her dreams, she never thought this could happen to her.

"How long do I have left in this school?" she asked, her voice coming out low and sad.

"I think till the end of this week, although I'll ask Mr Boyle if you can continue till the end of the school year. That's till June. And we'll somehow manage the school fees."

"No, you won't, Dad," said Zara firmly. "We need every last coin for the operation. If I have to change schools, I will. I'll learn to adjust. And I can make new friends."

She said this with a lump in her throat, "It's OK, Dad. I know how tense and hard it is for you both to get all that money."

She ran to her room and lay on her bed and shut her eyes tight. She heard Dad saying, "I'm a failure. I've let down my family." What was happening to her little world? They had been so happy, even if they had very little money, even with her sight problem, but now everything was breaking apart.

It wasn’t true, what Joom said, that if you had a pure heart and good intentions, nothing bad could touch you. Why, her Dad was the purest-hearted, the most devoted of teachers, and see what he was going through! She was too sad to even cry, but lay staring at the ceiling, which looked like a grey sea closing down on her.

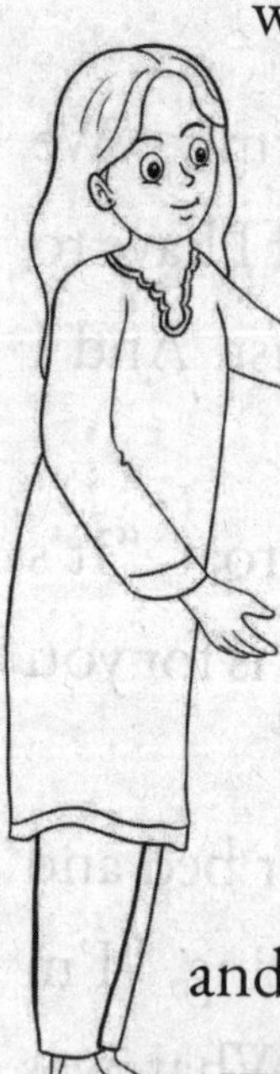

Mom came a short while later with a glass of golden milk. Ever - practical Mom, always putting her family first.

Drink this up,” she told Zara. “It’s grandma’s recipe. It’ll help you relax.”

Zara knew of this famous golden milk and the special herbs that went into it. It was a family recipe of Mom’s, something she had learnt from her mother, who in turn had learnt it from her mother; a generational cure-all for many ills; aching bodies, broken bones, toothache, insomnia, even broken hearts.

Zara had heard Mom pounding away in the kitchen. She knew some of the things that went into this secret milk—cloves, black pepper, cinnamon, anise. There were twelve spices in all, plus a generous spoon of yellow turmeric and a big dollop of honey. Zara sat up in bed and drank the entire glassful in one big gulp. It was soothing and delicious. Mom tucked her again into bed as if she were a small baby, and soon, Zara fell into a deep sleep.

When she woke up after a few hours, she felt much better until she remembered the events of that morning.

"You better have some lunch," said Mom when Zara walked into the dining room.

"Where's Dad?" Zara asked.

"He's gone out. You're free to do what you like today. You want to watch TV? Or should we go out together, go to the mall and do some window-shopping?"

Zara shook her head listlessly. Poor Mom! She was trying so hard to be nice to her, to soften that horrible piece of news.

"No, Mom. I'll just read my library book. I've got 'Harry Potter and the Goblet of Fire'. Don't worry about me, Mom."

Mom nodded. "I'll get on with my corrections and preparation then," she said. "Plus rustle up something for the night."

A quick lunch. Zara found she had lost all her appetite, and for once, Mom didn't insist on her finishing what was on her plate. The hours dragged on until it was bedtime. Dad returned and shut himself in his room. Zara settled under the quilt and Mom came in and smoothed down her tousled hair.

"Can I have some of that golden milk, Mom?"

"Of course. The spices are ready. I'll get you some."

She gulped it down. She didn't want to wake up soon. She fell asleep again. It was 11 pm when she awoke. The events of the day came rushing back to her. It had been the best day of her life and the worst. Her head felt heavy with all that sleep.

Joom! Of course, she would tell Joom everything. He must be waiting for her outside. She tiptoed out of bed and opened the balcony door very slowly so that it wouldn't squeak. She was glad she'd taken the trouble to oil the hinges earlier that week. Joom was there, seated in his usual place, his eyes closed.

"Joom!" she whispered as loudly as she could.

He got up with a jerk, rubbing his eyes with his big hands.

"Oh, it's you, little one," he said. "I did peep in through your window yesterday, but you were fast asleep. And today too. I thought maybe you didn't want to be friends with me any longer."

"Oh, no Joom," said Zara. "So much has happened. It's been the worst day of my life today."

She told him everything, from winning the quiz and the special prize, and Mr Boyle's meanness, to the devastating news Dad had broken to her that morning that she had to leave her school. "And I still don't know if we'll be able to go for the operation, Joom," she said. She told him everything matter-of-factly. Like it was a report for her school newspaper. There was no point in crying.

"Dad says he'll take a bank loan, but I don't know if he'll get so much money from the bank. And I don't want my parents to work so hard for the rest of their lives, taking tuitions, saving every bit of money and forgoing all luxuries. Joom, I just don't know what to do."

Zara couldn't say anything more. She sat, head in hands, staring blindly into space. Joom gave her a pat. "There's always a way, little one. There's always a way out."

Hardly had the words been spoken, when Zara felt herself being pulled into the air, and some sharp claws digging into her back. "Help! Help!" she cried, as she was lifted up into the dark skies, and felt the rush of air from powerful wings. She saw Joom in the balcony, his mouth a big circle of horror.

"It's Gorgonzola!"

At this, a sharp, guttural voice spoke, "So, I've finally found you, slave! I've been watching you two the last few days, cosying up and so happy and content. And you're bold enough to call me by name! Slave, do you realise you have run away from your master?"

"Drop her!" Joom shouted. "I'll come back and be your slave. But leave the little girl."

At this, the bird gave a horrible, mocking laugh. "Hahahaha! So, the slave thinks I have to obey him! No, slave, you are following the two of us, and I'm going to keep both of you as my slaves. Besides, you were pretty useless and didn't know much magic. This one looks bright. She will be useful to me." And again, he gave a cackle, and flew into the night air, holding Zara with his claws.

Zara saw the buildings and trees become smaller and smaller. She hadn't worn her glasses, but knew they were flying higher and higher into the skies as the air became colder and the buildings became a black blotch.

"Leave me, you ugly creature, leave me!" she shouted. But the bird laughed, a guttural laugh.

"You won't be alone," he said. "Your genie friend is running after us. That's the best way of catching him. I knew he'd never give up on you." And he cackled like a wicked witch, his voice now high-pitched and mocking.

◆◆◆

Chapter 24

Into the Pit of Evil

Zara's voice stuck in her throat as they flew higher and higher in the air. Far below, she could make out the black shadow of Joom scampering after her. But despite her terror, she had a warm, fuzzy feeling. Joom would not leave her. He'd be by her side, always. The skies grew darker and the air colder. Oh no! She was losing consciousness. Everything became black.

She woke up after what seemed many hours and blinked once or twice. The hard, bony claw of the bird was still gripping her clothes. The air became warmer, and the landscape below came closer. She could make out what looked like huge swathes of sand. She gulped. He had brought her into the middle of nowhere. The evil bird began descending to what looked like a gigantic sand dune with a dark, narrow opening.

Just before they touched ground, the bird let go, and Zara landed with a thud on soft sand. She heard heavy panting and looked up to see Joom in front of her, hiding her from the ugly, bird-like creature who looked like a vulture but was much uglier. Gorgonzola: a strange-looking bird with what looked like a black drooping moustache just above his beak. The Evil One.

"So, the two friends are here together," said the creature, and gave a loud cackle. And then, sharply to Joom, "Move aside, slave, so that I can see the girl. Or else I'll put both of you in chains."

Joom immediately moved aside. Zara was still on the ground, but she got up, brushing the sand off her clothes. She could feel the rough grains under her bare feet.

"How dare you kidnap me!" she shouted. "Don't think you can get away with this. My Mom and Dad will be calling the police. And once they find me, you'll be in jail, forever. Free us immediately, Gorgonzola! Joom is no longer your slave. He's my friend."

The creature let out another horrible cackle.

"Hahaha. So, this girl is feisty, I see. That makes things more interesting for me. I can see you are intelligent, but your friend is not too bright. You'll make a good combination, the two of you, to carry out my plans." He laughed, showing the insides of his horrible beak. A foul smell came out.

Then turning his attention to the genie, he said, "So slave, you thought you could hide from me forever? And you made a human friend? And you have the guts to call me by my name?" He spat out these words, so infuriated was he. "It's taken me over a thousand years to find you. And in the meantime, I've learnt the black arts. I know how to change my shape to resemble all the creatures that walk or fly or creep on the face of this earth. I just have to touch my moustache, and it's done."

Hardly had these words come out of his mouth, when the vulture reached out with its ugly clawed foot to touch the droopy black moustache and turned into a sweet-faced old grandmother like the ones you saw in nursery rhyme books, carrying a basket full of cookies and cupcakes. Only this grandmother had a droopy moustache.

"Like this, children?" the voice had changed too. It was an old lady's voice, gentle and quivery. "Oh, I forgot." The little lady peeled off the moustache and stuck it on her hand. "Like my magic moustache?" she cackled. "Ha-ha. But you both need to be more respectful and afraid of me."

So saying, the kind-looking granny again touched the moustache and turned into a desert lizard with two ugly horns on his brow. The droopy moustache was now just above the lizard's nose. He gnashed his teeth and laughed, seeing Zara's expression of absolute terror. Joom, too, took a step back.

"This human will be very useful to me," he said, almost to himself, swishing his scaly tail. "She appears to be a clever girl too, and I can take her with me to fool all my enemies. I can make her do things that she wouldn't know she was capable of doing. Hmmm." He looked at Zara with his dark, beady lizard eyes. "Now, the two of you better go inside my cave. I've got the urn all ready for you, slave, and there's another one for the girl too. But first, I want to eat. It's been a long flight. Go on in, now. March."

Zara and Joom walked in through the narrow opening in the sand dune. Joom held tight onto Zara's hand. She scrunched up her eyes to see better. Inside was a huge hollow all done up like a proper house. There was a sofa-set and a dining table and an enormous four-poster bed with satin pillows piled up on it. The kitchen had large cauldrons and saucepans and ladles hanging from hooks, and a furnace with red embers.

But the resemblance to a house ended here. On the wall were skeletons and skulls, both human and animal, and an especially ugly one of a human body with a lizard face. And up above, dangling from the high ceiling, was a chandelier made of grinning human skulls. Despite her failing eyesight, Zara could make all this out. She was terrified but tried not to show it. That would only make the Evil One happier, she knew.

"Hahaha," croaked Gorgonzola, "feel afraid, girl? Think this blubbering genie is going to protect you? Well, think again. See what I have for the two of you."

He gestured with his ugly head towards two large urns lying sideways, their stoppers next to them. "That's where each of you will go," he said, all his sharp teeth visible in his lizard face. "But first, I want to eat. But, just to make sure that you both don't try to escape, I'm going to put you in a stench tent. You won't be able to see or do anything because you'll be closing your eyes tight and holding your noses against the smell of rats and skunks and sewers. Hahahaha. Enjoy the smells!"

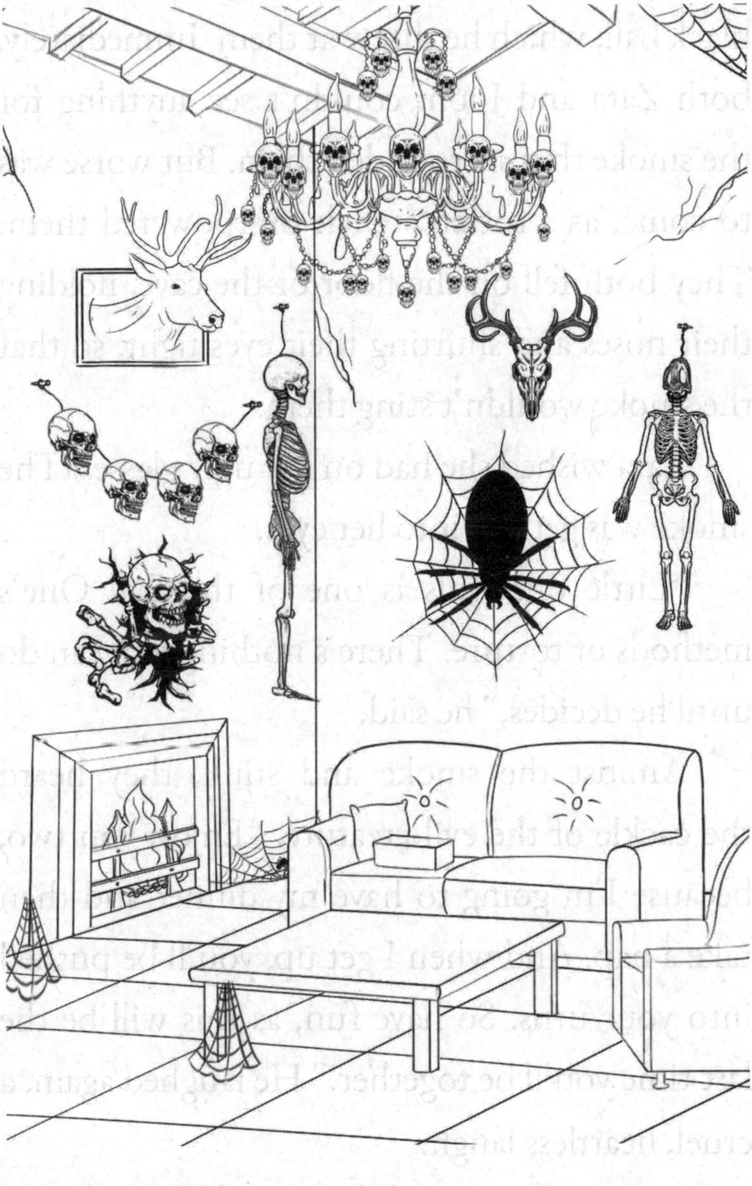

So saying, the lizard pulled out something from one of the kitchen cupboards. It was a small, black ball, which he threw at them. Immediately, both Zara and Joom couldn't see anything for the smoke that surrounded them. But worse was to come, as a rotten stench overpowered them. They both fell on the floor of the cave, holding their noses and shutting their eyes tight, so that the smoke wouldn't sting them.

Zara wished she had on her ugly glasses. The smoke was getting into her eyes.

"Little one, this is one of the Evil One's methods of torture. There's nothing you can do until he decides," he said.

Amidst the smoke and stink, they heard the cackle of the evil creature. "Enjoy, you two, because I'm going to have my dinner and then take a nap. And when I get up, you'll be pushed into your urns. So have fun, as this will be the last time you'll be together." He laughed again, a cruel, heartless laugh.

"Joom, I think I'm going to faint with the smell," said Zara. She held on to Joom with one hand, clutching her nose with the other and breathing heavily.

"Little human, what's happening to you?" Joom said in alarm.

There was no answer. Zara collapsed onto the floor.

◆◆◆

Chapter 25

Surprises Galore

Holding on to his nose with one hand, Joom tried to pick up Zara with the other. It wasn't easy as the smoke and the stink were getting worse.

"Little human, what's happened to you? Are you dead?" he stood above her in a state of agony, pleading with her to get up once again, as she lay lifeless on the floor.

"Wake up, little one, wake up," he said. But she lay still, eyes shut, inert.

Big, fat tears started rolling out of Joom's eyes. "Oh, little one, what have I got you into? What did I do to you? You've landed up here only because of my friendship with you. Oh, how I wish I hadn't made friends with you that first day when I saw you outside in your balcony. I should've stuck to my tree. I should've just minded my business. Now, all because of me, you've gotten yourself into this trap, this horrid cave, and into the clutches of this vile monster. And now you're dead!"

Joom's chest was heaving, streams of salty tears were pouring out of his scrunched-up eyes, and all the while, he was holding his nose with one of his hands and taking little gasps of air. Joom's tears were huge tears. They were bigger than human tears, almost ten times bigger. Like big marbles made of water. They fell on Zara's face and hair, *plip-plop, plip-plop*. They splashed all over her, making her clothes wet. Some fell into her eyes, which were slightly open.

A teardrop went in and she fluttered her eyes slightly, like when water gets into your eyes when you're showering. Joom was crying so hard, his body shaking, that he didn't notice. Then one of the tears fell on her nose and into her nostrils.

"A-a-choo!" Zara sat up, and immediately held her nose. She blinked, seeing the smoke around her. Joom gave a big smile (still holding his nose).

"Oh, you're alive! You're alive!" If it weren't for the smoke and the stench, he would have done a little dance.

Zara looked at him with half-closed eyes. "What happened?" she asked.

"Oh, I'm so glad you're not dead, little one,"

replied Joom. “You’d fainted with the vile smell.”

Everything came back to Zara with a whoosh—how she was picked up by the vulture-creature, taken to the sand-dune cave, and how the wicked bird turned into a kind-looking old lady and then a desert lizard and threw them both into a stink tent.

“Oh, you silly, of course I’m not dead,” said Zara, holding onto her nose. “Thanks to your tears, I woke up.”

Joom’s tears had stopped now. Zara looked at him and then felt her clothes. She was in her pyjamas, an old and comfortable pair with little fairies and sprigs of violets and roses patterned all over it. “Oh, goodness Joom, you’ve made my pyjamas all wet with your tears. You silly-billy, couldn’t you see I was breathing?”

Joom started crying again when he heard this. “You’re alive. That’s all that matters.”

Again, plop, a huge tear hit her nose and she let out another big sneeze.

"Oh dear," she whispered. "Gorgonzola will hear me. We better keep still."

"He's busy eating," said Joom. "I know his habits. When he's eating, he doesn't think of anything else. I can see him."

Through the smoky haze, Zara could make out an ugly lizard shape chomping on something slimy and slushy. The lizard then opened a big jar that was beside him, and a tiny kitten mewed and jumped out. It tried to run away, but the lizard caught hold of it with his long tongue, and tossed the little creature into the air.

The kitten mewed in terror. The lizard tried to catch the kitten again on his extended tongue, but the droopy moustache got in his way, and the poor creature fled into a corner.

"Hrrrmph!" he growled. "This moustache

is a nuisance." With one claw, he peeled it off and stuck it to the end of his tail. It looked like a sinister black bow. He then proceeded with his cat-and-mouse game, only that this time the poor kitten was the mouse.

"This is how the Evil One likes his dinner. Fresh, and full of fear. He told me once that when an animal is scared and runs and is then caught and eaten, its meat is tastier."

Zara watched in disgusted fascination as the kitten sped across the room, but was caught each time by the lizard. Finally, with one horrid crunch, it bit into the poor creature with its sharp black teeth and then swallowed it whole.

"Oh my goodness!" Zara caught hold of Joom's hand as tight as she could hold. Joom, thinking she'd faint once again, held her even more tightly.

"Little one, he will fall asleep now," he said, "and he'll sleep for a long time."

The two of them continued watching the ugly creature as he stretched himself out, his pink tongue lolling out, and the moustache still attached to the end of his tail.

◆◆◆

Chapter 26

A Narrow Escape

Zara continued holding on to Joom's hand, not uttering a word.

"He's too full to drag himself to his bed," said Joom. "Hasn't changed a bit these last thousand years."

Zara blinked. The ugly creature's feet were spread out, and his stomach bulged with the heavy dinner. She looked around. The room was still hazy with smoke. She could make out a small black ball, with smoke fizzing out of it. She looked at Joom. His eyes were scrunched

up and he had closed his nostrils with one hand, only removing it now and then to breathe.

Zara did not say anything. Was she imagining all this? Smoke was fizzing out of the ball as if it were a coke bottle that had been shaken vigorously and then opened. Gorgonzola's snores were getting louder. He was in the deepest of deep sleeps. She gently kicked the ball, and it rolled away to one side. The smoke became less.

"Joom," she whispered, "let's go. He's asleep." Joom, who was trying his best to not breathe, did not hear her the first time. "Come on. We have our chance now. Let's go."

Joom looked around. The lizard was still snoring.

"Little one, we can't. You don't know Gorgonzola. If he finds us leaving, he'll catch us and do terrible things to us." Then he noticed that the smoke—and the stench—was less.

"I can breathe much better," he told Zara.

"How did this happen?"

"I kicked it away," whispered Zara. "The stink ball. It's there, in that corner." She pointed to a spot about ten feet away. "Now, Joom, we've got to leave this cave before he wakes up."

Joom shook his head, his eyes round orbs of terror. "We can't escape, little human," he said. "We're in his clutches. Once you're under his control, that's it."

Zara looked at him very sternly. "Joom, No, we HAVE to try. I can see the exit from here. C'mon, Joom. You have to be brave."

But the genie just sat down on the ground, refusing to budge. Zara saw that her words had no effect on him. Time was running out. It was Zara this time who caught hold of his hand, trying to calm him. "I've got an idea. Joom, will you help me? It's our last chance."

Joom nodded.

"Joom, is there any way we can get Gorgonzola into the urn? Like what he planned for us?" It was better to give Joom a concrete plan to work on.

"How will we do that?" Joom was still quaking.

"Tell me, where is his food kept?"

"It's there, in that big cauldron. All the dead insects, dead rats and snakes. That's the smell he uses in these stink bombs. He loves the smell. It's evil like him."

"OK, then, show me."

Quietly, Joom took her to the cauldron, which was ten feet away from the sleeping lizard. When he opened the lid, the same stink-ball stench hit their nostrils. Zara looked at the putrid black-brown, slimy mess. Her stomach turned as the smell hit her. But she pulled herself together.

"Listen carefully, Joom. I'll lead the evil Gorgonzola towards the urn by holding out some of the food near his nose. Once he enters the urn, you have to push the rest of him inside and close it as quick as possible. When he's inside, he'll no longer get the smell and wake up. But it'll be too late. He'll be trapped. Can you do it?"

Joom again nodded, his body quivering.

Zara took a ladle of the evil-smelling stuff and held it in front of the lizard's nose. Just as she expected, he sniffed it in his sleep, and his tongue came out. It was a long orange tongue with tiny bumps and nodules. Zara knew from her science lessons that a lizard's tongue could extend to twice the size of its body. She'd seen the horrible creature's long tongue throwing up the terrified kitten and then catching it.

When Gorgonzola sniffed the food, she quickly moved ahead, so that he also had to move forward in his sleep, following the stench, his long, greedy tongue lolling out. It was a long, slow journey. Zara did not want to arouse any suspicion. Bit by bit, she and Gorgonzola reached the mouth of the urn. Zara sent up a small prayer. She thought of Mom and Dad, and how much they loved her. One more step and their ordeal would be over.

But just as Zara was about to hold the ladle near the mouth of the urn, Gorgonzola opened one eye, and was dazed to see Zara in front of him. Joom dived towards the fizzing stink bomb and threw it near Zara. The lizard, seeing the smoke, closed his eye again. "Must be a dream," he said, and continued snoring.

Zara's heart was hitting her rib cage. They waited for some minutes until the snores became deeper, and Joom kicked the stink bomb away. It was now or never. Zara held the ladle once again near the mouth of the urn, and the lizard moved towards it, his tongue sticking out. She threw the ladle with the foul mix inside the urn, and the ugly creature first pushed his tongue in and then most of his body. He was more than three-fourths of the way in when he got stuck. His bulging belly was too broad to go through the opening.

Zara and Joom acted in unison, and pushed with all their might. It was hard work, but the genie was big and strong. Zara hated touching the creature's rough, cold body, but she put all thoughts aside and did what she had to do. Gorgonzola, knowing something was amiss, was now awake, and let out a roar.

"Quick, Joom, the stopper."

Joom grabbed it and pushed it into the mouth of the urn. A little bit of the lizard's tail with the droopy black moustache was hanging out. It thrashed about as if it had a life of its own, the moustache making it look like a writhing black snake.

"Joom, don't let him escape!" Zara yelled. "His tail is out. He can escape."

The roaring from inside increased. The bit

of the tail that was out wriggled and thrashed about, and the stopper loosened.

"Joom, go grab a live coal," yelled Zara.

Joom ran towards the burning embers below the cooking pot and with the tongs, he pulled out a glowing coal and threw it on the thrashing tail. It landed perfectly. The moustache first caught fire, and then the tail; both turned a bright orange and then became black. All that was left was ashes. There was such a loud roar from the vile creature that the skeletons and the chandelier and all the pots and pans shook. But the tail was burnt to a cinder.

Zara used all her strength to push the stopper in firmly. With one bound, Joom jumped across the room and pushed it in further, so that there was no chance of it ever opening. Gorgonzola was well and truly trapped within. She and Joom could hear him thrashing about inside the walls of the urn, but there was no chance for him to escape. The walls were made of a special metal that could never be broken. He couldn't even change his shape because the moustache too had been burnt.

They looked at each other in amazement.

"Joom, we've done it," said Zara, her eyes wide and shining.

They gave each other high-fives. It took Joom a little longer to realise that he was now free of the Evil One. He put his ear close to the walls of the urn, and gave a big guffaw of laughter.

"Gorgonzola, you're trapped forever. No one will ever find you here," he yelled.

"Wait and see, you slave! You have the guts to address me by my name, I see, as if you are equal to me.I'll get you both, you and the girl, and tear you limb by limb and eat you. You can't do this to me." Gorgonzola's voice came from the urn as if from the bottom of a deep well.

"Hahaha," laughed Joom, dancing in joy. "It's my turn to laugh. You'll rot in hell and die the death you deserve. Here's my last gift to you."

So saying, Joom began making explosive armpit farts. "That's what you get, you wicked man. You're like a stinking piece of old cheese, like your name. And you can get mouldier in that urn."

Zara gave Joom two small punches. "Joom, stop it. Stop being so childish. Let's just get out."

She had to finally drag Joom away, and the two walked out of the narrow opening and into the soft desert sands. A huge boulder, as big as an SUV, was lying nearby. Joom looked at it.

"Little one, I remember some of my magic. It's coming back to me. Let me try."

So saying, he uttered a few magic words under his breath. To Zara's amazement, he gave the boulder a small push and it rolled effortlessly and lodged itself in the opening.

"Joom, you did it! You got back your magic!"

Joom gave a modest bow, looking very pleased with himself. "No one will ever find him there," he said. "And even if he ever manages to get out of the urn, which he won't, he'll be stuck in that cave. Even a Tyrannosaurus Rex won't be able to move that rock."

Zara looked around her. All she wanted was to go home. "We have to get back, Joom. We're in the middle of nowhere."

"Don't you worry, little Zara," said Joom. "We're not far from home. Let me carry you, because your feet are too small for crossing this sand. So saying, he lifted Zara up and made her sit on his shoulders and she held on to his ears for support. He took a few big steps, and soon, Zara could see the outline of her building in the distance. And then something hit her, something so amazing that she almost stopped holding Joom's ears. No, no! She couldn't believe it. No, this couldn't be true.

◆◆◆

Chapter 27

It's a Miracle

Zara held on tighter to Joom's ears, and looked about her. There it was, her building, the only one with a huge tamarind tree growing in front of it. It was dark, so the tree was a dark shadow, but she could make out every little thing. There were one or two lights on the floors above her house. She looked up at the sky and there was the yellow moon, to all intents and purposes looking as if it were smiling at her. Her heart gave a huge, happy thump.

SUPER MARKET
ISH

Earlier, when she made out the lizard and the black stink ball, and Joom's kind face, she hadn't had time to think, or even realise that she could now see. But now—

Still, Zara wanted to be sure. Joom walked down the quiet streets, and she could see every lamppost, and read the names of the shops. There was Kabab House, the restaurant from where Mom sometimes ordered lunch when she was too tired to cook; there was the community park where she sometimes went to play in the evenings. It was night-time, but every object was visible to her. She blinked and closed her eyes and then opened them, expecting the usual fuzzy vision, but no, she could see every sharp detail.

"Joom," she held his ears tight. "Guess what! I can see!"

Joom didn't seem to realise what she was saying.

"We'll be home in a minute, little Zara."

"Joom, I can read the signs on the shops. I can see Balaji Supermarket. That's where Mom orders her groceries. And next to it Kishmish Ice-creams."

Joom stopped in his tracks. "You can see now?"

Zara hugged him while sitting on his big shoulders. "Yes, you dumbo-bumbo. That's what I'm saying."

Joom tossed her into the air and caught her, and they both laughed so hard that somewhere, a light came on.

"Shhh," said Zara, as Joom went into the shadows. They both giggled.

"I told you, miracles happen."

"I believe you, I believe you," sang Zara.

By then, Zara's building, the tallest and shabbiest building on the street but the only one with a huge tamarind tree in front of it, loomed up ahead of them.

"We're home. Home sweet home."

"In you go," said Joom, pushing her into the balcony. "Go and get some sleep."

"I can see, I can see," sang Zara.

"Shhh," said Joom. "You don't want to wake your parents and the entire neighbourhood, do you? See, what I told you came true. Miracles do happen."

◆◆◆

Chapter 28

A Whole New World

That night, Zara lay on her bed, staring at all the familiar objects in her room that she could now distinguish without those heavy glasses. It was so wonderful to see with her naked eyes. The table she worked on, her old stuffed toys, the little bookcase with her school books neatly stacked on one shelf and below, books by her favourite authors JK Rowling and Roald Dahl.

Why, she could read every name on the cover from this distance. The Harry Potter books were in order, starting from the first book, 'The

Philosopher's Stone', up to the last, 'Harry Potter and the Deathly Hallows'. Her cupboard door was a little ajar, and her new red dress lay neatly hanging.

She looked out of the window at the tamarind tree. It was as dark and bushy as ever, with the stick-like giant pods swaying gently in the breeze. She could see Joom lounging on one of its branches, a black shadow against the darkness.

There was no point in trying to sleep. She quietly swung out of bed and opened her balcony door a crack. "Joom," she whispered. "What are you up to?" Then, she went and danced a little jig in the balcony. "Joom, I can see, I can see!"

"Yes, little one, I told you to have faith."

"And I owe it to you, Joom."

Joom got off the tree and spread himself in his usual place, his back to the wall. "And how did I help?"

"Your tears, Joom, your tears. That was what cleared up my bad vision. You have magic in your tears."

Joom gave a big, goofy smile. "I don't know about that, but I'm glad to be of help." Then, on a sober note, he said, "I honestly gave you up as dead and gone." A little teardrop fell from the corner of his eye.

"Oh, Joom, you have the kindest and purest heart. And see, you're no longer a genie without any magic. You cured me."

"I did." Joom said, his voice full of wonder. "And I even used magic to move that huge boulder. Little one, I feel so much better, so much more powerful, so much more like a genie. I think my magic has returned."

"Why are you so unsure? Of course it's returned, you silly-billy," said Zara. "All you had to do was to try. It's just the beginning, Wait and see, it'll only get better." Then, on another note, she said, "I can't wait to tell Mom and Dad that I can now see properly. We won't need the operation. I'd like to see their faces when I tell them. How surprised they'll be."

"They certainly will, my friend," said Joom, and the two of them did a little dance, jumping about and clapping hands very quietly in the balcony.

"But I want to keep it a surprise for my friends. Oh dear!" Zara clapped her hands over her mouth. "If I wear those glasses to school, how will I be able to see, now that my vision is normal?"

"Hmm," said Joom. "Now, let me see if I can do some magic. Give me those glasses."

Zara ran back into her room and brought the glasses out.

"Here you are."

Joom held them up and closed his eyes, muttering some spells under his breath. Zara tried hard to listen, but couldn't understand a word. Then he tossed the glasses up into the air and caught them deftly.

"Here, now try."

Zara put the glasses on her nose, and found she could still see perfectly.

"How did you do that? These are no longer powered but just plain see-through glasses. And they're also so light."

Joom grinned. "I've got it back, my magic. That's for sure."

"You bet you have," said Zara, giving Joom a hug. "Otherwise, I'd never have been able to see—and my secret would be out, if I go to school minus my specs."

"Did you know, little human, that you're one brave girl? If it weren't for your courage, we'd both be trapped in those urns."

They both became a little quiet, thinking of the horrible adventure they'd had together, and their narrow escape.

"You know, Joom, you're a real true friend. I heard you shouting at Gorgonzola when he picked me up. You said to leave me and take you instead."

"My little friend," said Joom, "if anything had happened to you, I don't think I could ever forgive myself."

Zara nodded. "I'm so happy, Joom. But there's still one thing that makes me sad. Dad getting fired. I know how much he's done for the school, and he doesn't deserve to be sacked. It's just not fair."

"Yes, little Zara. We have to do something about that. But you better go to bed now. You need all the sleep you can get. And tomorrow, we can think what to do about your Dad's dismissal."

◆◆◆

Chapter 29

Mr Boyle Is at It Again

Zara was deep in sleep the next morning when Mom came in to wake her up.

"Get up, Zara, we have to leave," she said, shaking Zara gently.

She got up, rubbing her eyes. Mom reached out for her glasses and put them on her.

"Mom, I can see," said Zara, taking them off.

"OK," said Mom, putting them back on her nose. "That's very good. Go and get ready."

"But Mom—"

Mom had already left the room. Oh no!

Nothing had registered. She probably thought Zara was waking up from a nice dream. Quickly, Zara brushed her teeth and wore her uniform. She'd taken off her glasses, and it felt so strange to not be looking through a thick lens. She was ready in record time, again popped the glasses back on, and went to have her breakfast. Mom was in the kitchen, packing their lunches and Dad was sitting and staring into space. They'd already had breakfast, and Zara's toast and egg lay on her plate.

"Dad, I can see," she told him, taking off her glasses.

Dad gave her a strange look. "Hurry and finish your breakfast. It's getting cold."

Oh no! Even he didn't believe her. She finished eating and went to wash her hands. She heard them talking to each other in lowered tones.

"The poor girl has lost her mind. She doesn't want to leave the school. That's why she's saying she can see."

"I can never ever forgive Boyle for this. Never."

It was a gloomy party that set out for school that morning. Mom's face was tear-streaked, and Dad's was grey and dull. Zara sat at the back, glad neither of her parents could see her and notice her excitement. She was longing to point out all the familiar sights on their journey. Earlier, these had been a blur—trees, people, buildings, vehicles—but now, she could make out all the details, the makes of the cars, the crowded buses with people hanging out of the door, the auto-rickshaws that didn't seem to obey any of the traffic rules, the scooters and the pedestrians. Driving in Delhi was crazy, Dad often said, and she understood why.

Then, a long white car with a snooty-looking driver wearing a peaked cap drew up alongside them at the traffic signal. A fashionable lady was sitting behind with a fluffy white dog on her lap. Zara stared. The dog's hair above its face was tied back with a little pink satin ribbon. The lady caught her staring and gave her a little smile, lifting the dog to show her. Zara smiled back, and then the lights changed, and the car zoomed away.

When they approached the better part of the city, where Summerdale High School was located, the roads became broader, and there were flowering trees on either side. It was so pretty! Zara savoured the sight. It was not that she had never seen this earlier—her old heavy glasses helped her see things but now she noticed each and every little thing. It was like she had woken up to a new life.

Oh, why didn't Dad and Mom believe her? She'd tried again, while they were taking the stairs to get into their car, but they just told her to hurry. "Not that Boyle can do any more damage to me, and give me another red mark," Dad said darkly, "but let's be on time. We don't want the only earning member to also lose her job." Mom, who was carrying a bag of books, turned to look at him and a little tear rolled out of her eye. But she said nothing. They were so caught up in their sorrow.

I'll read out something to them this evening, thought Zara to herself. *Without wearing these glasses. Then they'll know. It's as if they're deaf and haven't even heard me.*

Zara couldn't take the gloomy silence in the car. "Mom, Dad, will Mr Boyle call me and Ramu up on stage today? Will he announce to the school that we've won the cup?" There was silence. "I mean, now that I have to leave the school, will he go through with all this?"

"Yes, child, he will," responded Mom mechanically. "It's a feather in the cap for the school, and he'll take all the credit."

Dad remained quiet.

Her parents were lost in thought. Despite her happiness, Zara felt her heart twinge when she saw how beaten they looked. No, she had to do something about this.

"I have some very good news for all of you," said Mr Boyle, his egg-face cracking into a smile. "Some very good news." It was the Monday morning assembly, and the entire middle and senior school were seated in the big auditorium. A bigger and grander auditorium was being built in the land adjacent to the school. Adam Butt's father had contributed very generously towards the building.

The children, especially the seniors, waited with bated breath. They'd all learnt of the win and were expecting some kind of celebration.

"I'm sure you've already heard that our school won the cup for the Junior Science Talent Quiz. It was a very close call, but our two stars, Ramu Damodaran and Zara Kumar, managed to pull off the win and took the cup. Here it is." Mr Boyle held up the heavy silver cup that had been polished to a gleam. The students gasped and then cheered.

"I'd like our two champions to come up on stage. Ramu of grade 7 and Zara of grade 6, please come up."

They both came up. Zara remembered that she had to walk slowly; no one yet knew of her miraculous recovery. Ramu walked beside her and helped her up the stairs to the stage.

"I want to congratulate both of you for bringing back the cup to our school. Students, give them a big clap."

The entire assembly clapped loudly, and there were cheers for Ramu from his boisterous classmates, and some for Zara too.

Mr Boyle turned to the students after the applause had died down. He smiled at them. Zara could see her parents, who were seated along with the other teachers, turn and give a worried look to one another. Her stomach gave a lurch.

"These two students have worked very hard.

Ramu's father is a scientist and his mother a computer scientist. He's done both his parents proud, and our school proud too. Now, this girl Zara, hmmm." Mr Boyle gave her his frog-eyed look. "Aren't you Dr Sameer's daughter?" he asked, pretending not to know.

"Yes, Mr Boyle, sir," said Zara.

"Oh, such a pity about your father," he said, and then clapped his hand over his mouth as if he had mistakenly said the wrong thing.

The students began tittering. Adam Butt and some other boys started saying, "Boo to Dr Sameer." They began giving loud hoots.

Mr Boyle pretended to be angry. "Boys and girls, this is not the way to behave. Enough of this noise."

But the students knew when Mr Boyle did not mean things in earnest, and continued booing. Zara, her face red, and tears running down her cheeks, walked off the stage. She didn't have to pretend she couldn't see. She really couldn't, with the tears falling in a steady stream. Mom was waiting below, and pulled her away outside.

Mom held her firmly and half-walked, half-carried her to Dad's office where they could be alone.

"Mom, I won the cup for the school. Why did Mr Boyle do this to me?"

Mom, who was usually so careful with her words, gave vent to her anger. "He's just a low-down, vicious and virulent monster who's not fit to be a headmaster. How can he do this to an eleven-year-old child!"

Just then, Dad walked in, his face purple. Zara ran to him, crying.

"Dad, I want to leave this school right now. I don't want to ever come here again."

"Don't you cry, my precious," said Dad, wiping her tears with his checked handkerchief. "That was his way to get back at me."

"Dad, you can't take this lying down! You

have to take action. Go and tell the board of governors how he's behaved. Tell them it's all lies, that you never yelled at Adam Butt and stopped him from writing his exam."

Dad looked at her sadly. "Child, what can I say? Tell them that the students booed? That will look so silly. And then, there are those signatures from those students who testify that I am constantly attacking the Butt boy. What leg do I have to stand on?"

Before Zara could reply, the door burst open.

◆◆◆

Chapter 30

An Apology

Dickie Douglas stood breathing heavily, tie askew and hair dishevelled. His big ears seemed to be sticking out even more. For a few moments, he stood there not saying anything, just trying to get his breath back, as Zara glared at him. This was the boy who'd pretended to beat her with a stick and who'd joined Adam Butt's gang in bullying her.

"Dickie, what can I do for you?" Dad said. Zara now glared at Dad. She wanted to tell him not to be nice to Dickie. He didn't know about the earlier incident. He only pitied Dickie for being humiliated at the assembly.

"Sir, I have something to tell you."

"Sit down, son, and here, drink this water." Dad handed him a cold bottle from his mini fridge.

"Thank you, sir," said Dickie, and downed the entire bottle in one gulp. His hands were shivering. "Sir, sorry I barged in, without even knocking. But I didn't want anyone to see me enter."

"That's OK, son. Take your time. I have all the time for you. Do you want Zara and her mom to leave the room? Is it something private?"

Zara ground her teeth but kept quiet. Dad was always putting his students first, even when he was leaving. Dickie looked up and saw Zara's malignant look.

"No, sir, that's OK."

He sat silent for some more moments, while Dr Sameer waited patiently.

"Do you need help with your math? I won't be able to help you because Mr Matthew is now your teacher. You should ask him. It's against the school rules for me to help you."

"No sir, I don't need help. I just came to apologise to Zara for my behaviour last week. I'm sorry, Zara," he said, turning to her. "Honest, those boys wanted to have some fun at my expense. They threatened me—" He stopped, his face turning red.

Dickie took a big gulp and said in a rush. "They said if I didn't pretend to hit you and scare you, they'd pull off my trousers during the break and make me stand in my briefs."

For a moment, there was a stunned silence.

"This is very serious, son," said Dr Sameer. "You should complain to your class teacher."

"Sir, that's complicated. It's Adam Butt's group who did it. Even you couldn't go against them." He stopped, embarrassed. Perhaps he had said too much? Then he took another big gulp and said, "There's something more I have to tell you, sir. That petition that some of us signed—Mr Boyle forced us to sign it. Sir, many of us are terrified of him. Adam Butt's friends signed it happily, but there were others in the class who didn't want to sign it.

"Sir, we know what a good and fair teacher you are. But Mr Boyle threatened to suspend us or worse. He didn't make it clear. And the way he spoke, it was that we either sign or get thrown out of the school. He said the waiting list to join this school runs into hundreds."

Dad sat drumming his fingers on the table. Mom and Zara were about to say something when Dad gave a look that said to not interfere.

"Sir, there's one more thing," said Dickie. "It seems Adam Butt's father and Mr Boyle have had some kind of business agreement, and Mr Boyle is going to get a lot of money under the table."

"How do you know all this?" Dad's voice was sharp.

"Sir, Adam Butt's dad is my dad's boss. My dad's his personal assistant. So, he knows pretty much everything that's happening. When I told him how Mr Boyle had treated me last week, he was furious. But there was nothing he could do about it because he's not rich or important."

"Well, that doesn't help my case much," said Dad wryly.

"Sir, some of the students in my class are really angry that Mr Boyle treated Zara so badly today in assembly. But I heard Adam threatening them that if they said anything, he'd have them beaten up. But some of them said they would. That's what I came to tell you."

"I see," said Dad, scratching his nose. "But unless it actually happens—and we don't know if it ever will—things will remain as they are."

"No, Dad," Zara spoke up. They all turned to look towards her. She sat there, looking very still and firm. "Dad, you have to fight back. You can't allow Mr Boyle to run all over you." Zara was thinking of that first step she had taken to kick the stink ball out of the way. One step at a time; that was all that was needed. Dad could just try, not give up like this without trying.

"There's nothing much I can do, child," said

Dad. "All the evidence is circumstantial. Unless those students retract their statement, nothing changes. And I don't see that happening. Both Mr Boyle and Adam Butt's father will be exposed."

Zara thought quickly. There was no point in trying to convince her father. Time was running out. "OK Dad," she said, "we have very little time left in this school, the two of us. Can you leave it to me?"

Dad scratched his head, thinking. "I don't want you to do anything silly or dangerous. And, besides, what can you do?"

"I don't know right now, but let me try."

"Well, if you promise not to do anything silly—"

"Dad, have you ever seen me do anything silly?"

Dad shook his head.

"Well then," she said, giving her father a hug, "just trust me. Dickie, will you meet me tomorrow in the library? During recess?"

"Sure," said Dickie.

The two children and Mom went back to class, leaving Dad to pack up his books and belongings. As Zara left the room, she held her head high, not bothering about the whispers when people saw her. She had her friends, and there was Joom, her BFF. They'd set things right, or else her name was not Zara Kumar.

◆◆◆

Chapter 31

Something's Cooking!

"Oh my goodness! If it's not the quartet again." Miss Ray peered at the five students who'd come to the library – Zara, Mimi, Pixie, Ramu and Dickie. "Oh, I see it's a quintet now. Is there another quiz?"

"No, Miss," said Zara truthfully. Miss Ray was not considered regular staff, so hadn't attended the assembly the previous day. "We've come to discuss a project. An inter-class project," she added, in case Miss Ray wondered why now there were students from different grades working together.

"Well, you know the rules," said the librarian, going back to her reading. Zara saw it was another voluminous book, *A Little Life* by some hard-to-pronounce author. It was funny that such a big fat book had a title like this. It was hardly little!

The five of them once again took the table at the far end of the room so as not to disturb Miss Ray. Zara began talking in a low voice.

"Thanks so much for coming," she said. "You all know most of my story, but not everything."

"What a creep he is, Adam Butt," said Mimi angrily. "I hate Mr Boyle, I really hate him."

"Well, there's no point in getting all worked up," said Zara. "He's asking my Dad to pay my school fees. You know that Dad is exempted from paying because he does so much for the school. Now, Mr Boyle says that since he's leaving, how can they continue paying for me? And my parents just can't afford it.

"You mean?" Pixie's eyes filled with tears.

"Yes, Pixie and Mimi," said Zara. "I'll have to join a new school in the middle of a term. Of course, Mom and Dad said they'd plead with him to allow me to continue till the end of the school year. But—" she stopped, her voice choked in her throat.

"No, they can't do this to you," said Ramu.

"Well, they can and they are," said Zara. "The board is quiet about this."

"What about your operation?" Mimi's voice came out in a shocked whisper. Zara kept quiet. She hadn't yet told her friends of the miracle. If she told them how she got back her sight, she'd have to tell them about Joom too. And they'd think she'd gone bonkers.

"The Boiled Egg has it for you and your family," said Ramu soberly.

"Well, I've brought Dickie to this meeting because he has something new to add. Dickie, tell us everything you know."

Dickie, despite being with children younger than himself, flushed red as he had to speak.

"You all know that the students signed that petition saying Dr Sameer purposely stopped Adam Butt from writing his exam."

They nodded. Yes, everyone had heard of that.

"Well, this story has two parts. First of all, Mr Boyle forced us to sign it."

They all gasped.

"No way," said Ramu.

"Mr Boyle came to our class and told us what a bad man Dr Sameer was, and how he was always singling out Adam Butt. Then, he said he'd prepared a letter that we all had to sign, saying that we were all unhappy with Dr Sameer and didn't want him to teach us and also that he was a very unfair teacher."

"But surely some of you objected," said Ramu. "I mean, this is a bare-faced lie."

Dickie looked down, ashamed, and shook his head.

"You all actually joined in telling a lie?" Mimi asked, shocked.

"Mr Boyle threatened us with suspension,

even expulsion if we didn't sign. And Adam Butt has a gang of goons operating under him. They'd punch us if we disagreed."

"But still," said Ramu, "why didn't you stand up for the truth?" He looked accusingly at Dickie.

"Me?" Dickie asked. "You're telling me to stand up and voice my opinion?"

"Well, why not? You're doing it now, aren't you? You're telling us what actually happened. All you had to do was to go and tell the board what you told us. Or write them an anonymous letter."

Dickie shook his head. "How? I don't have any voice, and my dad is not rich or important."

Zara was reminded of Dad, and also Joom, who said much the same thing. They claimed they had no power. Now, Joom had learnt he did have a voice, he did have power. But Dad was still such a wimp.

"Dickie, you do have a voice," said Zara

gently. "You came and told Dad and me the actual truth of what happened. You are brave. You did the right thing."

Dickie looked at her gratefully. He seemed to grow a bit taller and sat straighter.

"OK, now. Tell us the second part of the story. You said the story had two parts," said Ramu.

"OK," said Dickie. "This is where it becomes interesting. Mr Chaudhury, Adam Butt's father, has opened a new luxury toilet paper factory. That's his latest venture." The children began giggling. Dickie continued, "Mr Chaudhury and Mr Boyle have struck a deal. It seems if the school orders their toilet paper from Mr Chaudhury, he'd pay Mr Boyle something under the table."

"What kind of toilet paper are they manufacturing?" Mimi asked curiously.

"It's called Butt Luxury Wipes," said Zara. "I overheard Mr. Solomon telling my Dad."

They started laughing, and Miss Ray looked up from her book.

"If you want to laugh and joke, you can go outside," she said sternly. "I thought you all were working on a project."

"Sorry, Miss Ray," said Zara, and they all lowered their voices.

"You know, my Dad used to help out with the accounts when Mr Dimpleby was headmaster. But when Mr Boyle took over, he told my Dad that he didn't need to do that job any longer. That's because my Dad would oversee all the purchases of the school. He planned everything out."

"What a devious plan," said Ramu.

"Zara, why didn't you tell us all this earlier?" Pixie asked.

"I only learnt about it recently. And I didn't want to tell you about the accounts stuff because I didn't understand it myself. And yesterday, I couldn't speak for sadness after the way Mr Boyle insulted me and my father. But now," and she looked at all of them with fire in her eyes, "I want revenge."

"Revenge?"

"My father's been treated so badly by Mr Boyle. I want to give him a taste of his own medicine," said Zara.

"And how will you do that?" Ramu asked.

"That's why I've come to you all for help. Will you all join me?"

"We will," they all said. Not loudly, but quietly and firmly so as not to attract Miss Ray's attention.

"OK then," said Zara. "Put on your thinking caps and let's come up with a plan. Tomorrow is Dad's last day and probably mine too. It's not clear. Dad did ask Mr Boyle to let me continue until the end of the term, but he didn't give a proper answer. And Mr Boyle is calling a farewell assembly where the entire middle and senior school have to attend. It's a special farewell assembly for Dad, like what we have when a teacher leaves after some years. He wants to give everyone the impression that he's being very fair. So, we have very little time."

Dickie cleared his throat. "I have to tell you something else," he said.

"What?" Zara asked.

"It's about this assembly. Mr Chaudhury is going to present your father a big bouquet. He's going to drop in sometime during that assembly tomorrow. He's supposed to be the chief guest of honour or something."

Zara was so furious that she almost banged on the table. "Mr Boyle's worse than scum!" she said through gritted teeth. "That's his way of humiliating my Dad even more."

"Yes, it's Mr Boyle's ultimate revenge," said Dickie. "He's going to have a good laugh seeing your dad's face when Mr Chaudhury walks in. He's even arranged a couple of videographers to film everything. I know because my dad was told to arrange the videographers and order a huge bouquet from the florist."

Pixie had to rub Zara on her back. She had gone red in the face and looked as if she were going to explode.

"Zara, don't freak out," said Mimi. "We'll think of something."

They sat around, lost in thought. Zara was quivering with rage. She knew all the things said about anger, that it prevented you from thinking clearly, and that you'd regret it later. But the Boiled Egg's ultimate revenge was too much to bear. Then she remembered something else she'd read about anger, that sometimes, just sometimes, anger was the tool that made you take the right kind of action. Yes, she'd use this as the motivation to take revenge on Dad's unfair dismissal.

But how?

Mimi was the first to break the silence. "I know," she said, "why don't the kids in Adam Butt's class bring placards saying they want their teacher back and it's all a lie?"

"Not possible," said Dickie. "They're terrified of Mr Boyle and of Adam Butt. No one will dare do this."

"OK, how about all of us writing an anonymous letter to the board, telling them what exactly happened?" Pixie asked.

"And who'd believe it?" Ramu asked. "A bunch of kids sending a letter? They'd throw it in the bin." They nodded. Yes, nobody'd believe them.

Ramu turned to Dickie, a spark in his eyes. "Dickie, tell me, when is this consignment of toilet paper being sent to the school? Do you know?"

"Today," said Dickie. "A thousand rolls."

"And do you know where they're being stored?" Ramu asked.

"The usual place. The store room in the basement."

"Okay," said Ramu. "I have a plan, but there are many loopholes in it."

"Tell us, Ramu," said Zara, her eyes shining. "What is the plan?"

Ramu told them. The five of them listened and discussed what they would do. There was only one hitch, which they couldn't find a solution to. But Zara smiled brightly. "It's an excellent plan. And leave it to me to take care of that hitch."

"What is the solution?" Ramu asked.

"Well, I can't tell you right now, but keep your fingers crossed that it'll all work out," said Zara.

"And thank you. You all are my true friends."

She wanted to give all of them a high-five, but Miss Ray was staring at them. "You all look very excited about your project," she said.

"Yes, Miss," said Zara, as they got up to leave. "We think it's a unique one." She and the others got up just as the bell rang, thanked Miss Ray, and left the library.

◆◆◆

Chapter 32

Revenge Is Sweet

The last day.

Zara got up that morning nice and early, her eyes sparkling with what lay ahead. In keeping with the earlier headmaster's tradition of giving a small farewell speech to the departing staff, Mr Boyle had called the entire middle and high school students and teachers to attend.

Dad didn't want any farewell. "I don't know what Boyle wants with all this—treating me like a dog and then this drama of saying how much I've done for the school."

"Well, don't show up," said Mom. "That would be the best thing to do. I won't go either. Even if I lose my job over this."

"Don't be foolish," said Dad. "We need your income now that I won't be having one. Besides, Boyle may do something more drastic if I don't show up."

"Like what?"

"Like cutting my dues. You know he has the last word."

Zara overheard her parents speaking. She didn't want to tell Mom and Dad about the nasty surprise awaiting him. Her whole body was tingling with anticipation when she thought over the plan they had hatched.

The students from grade 6 to grade 12 were all seated in the auditorium that morning. It was exciting for them to miss their morning class. A huge bunting hung over the top of the stage with the words 'Farewell to Our Dear Teacher'. This piece was pulled out every time a teacher left.

Zara was seated in the front row, between

Dad and Mom. When the family entered the auditorium, they cheered and stood up for him. Except for Adam Butt and his gang, all the other students respected Dr Sameer.

"Sir, please don't leave," said one of them. "We'll never get a teacher like you." If only they had cheered for her father earlier, when Mr Boyle was humiliating her. But then, Mr Boyle was up there on stage, controlling everything.

Mr Boyle strode onto the stage and shouted out, "Silence" in a terrible voice. Zara could see he didn't like anybody praising her father. She sat there, eyes shining, on tenterhooks, waiting for her plan to go through. She'd crossed the fingers of both hands and kept her legs crossed too, just for extra luck.

Mr Boyle had worn what looked like his most expensive suit, a black one with shiny gold buttons all the way down the front. The middle button was almost bursting. He cleared his throat and began.

"We're all gathered here today because one

of our oldest teachers, Dr Sameer, is leaving the school for better prospects. Most of you have been taught by him. I'm sure you'll all agree that

he is a very fine teacher. But unfortunately, he has to leave our school. But we want to give him a befitting farewell, which is why we are here. In fact, you can all see that this event is being videotaped." Everyone had noticed the big studio cameras at the front and the back of the hall with two professional videographers.

"Dr Sameer has taught students diligently, and has been a very gentle and refined teacher." He paused, waiting for Adam Butt and his group to disagree. But there was no answer from the boys. Zara turned to look at them, and was surprised to see even those boys looking a little sheepish. Only Adam Butt sat proudly, with a sncer on his face. He caught Zara looking at him, and had the grace to look down.

"Now," continued Mr Boyle, looking a little disappointed, "since Dr Sameer is such a special teacher, I've called over someone special to hand something to him—a very special gift." Mom and Dad looked at each other. Who was this someone special?

Just then, the squat, burly figure of Mr Chaudhury, Adam's father, was seen entering the hall. He strode in majestically, carrying an enormous bouquet of roses, lilies and carnations.

Just as he reached the middle of the stage where Mr Boyle stood, there were sudden loud sounds. Oh my goodness! These were fart sounds. *Phut! Phut! Phut!* They became louder and louder. Where on earth were they coming from? Definitely from the stage. Mr Butt looked aghast as the children began laughing.

But this was just the prelude. From the fly loft, the part of the stage high above from which scenery or angel figures were lowered, a pile of toilet paper rolls came raining down. Initially, no one knew what they were, and just gasped, looking upward. Then they saw the cover—Butt Extra-Soft Luxury Toilet Wipes. There were perhaps a hundred rolls, maybe even two hundred. They dropped down and rolled all over the stage. Some of them rolled off the stage and landed near the

Extra-Soft Luxury
Toilet Wipes
Extra-Soft Luxury
Toilet Wipes
Extra-Soft Luxury
Toilet Wipes

students. This was like a signal to them. They picked them up and tossed them around. The laughter reached the roof.

"Butt toilet paper. Soft and extra luxurious to wipe your butt," screamed the children. "Adam Butt, it's your dad's product, isn't it?" And they made loud, farty sounds. There was a proper uproar.

Mr Boyle looked stupefied. He stood there with his frog eyes bulging, his mouth hanging open. He opened and closed his mouth like a goldfish but no words came. This was not the case with Mr Chaudhury. His fleshy face grew red with rage. Some of the rolls hit him plonk on the head. The others were aimed at Mr Boyle's bottom.

"Mr Boyle, sir," the students screamed, "it's

like the toilet paper is begging you to use them and wipe your butt with them. You must have done a huge one, Mr Boyle."

"What is the meaning of this, Mr Boiled?" Mr Chaudhury shouted. "You mean to insult me? I am like toilet paper? Just because I manufacture it?"

"I-I-I—" Mr Boyle was literally lost for words.

"Mr Boyle. You made us sign that petition, didn't you? Dr Sameer caught Adam Butt cheating and that's why he stopped him from writing the paper. But you twisted it around and threatened us with expulsion."

Everyone looked in shock at a boy with big ears and big feet who'd walked right up on to the stage and pointed an accusing finger at Mr Boyle. As if on cue, the rest of the students started shouting.

"You forced us to sign the petition, Mr Boyle. Admit it. Adam Butt, out with the truth. You were cheating in the exams and you made up this cock-and-bull story."

Adam Butt, who'd also come up to the stage, probably to protect his father from the toilet rolls hitting him, looked at the shouting students. Zara saw the expression on his face, a look of sheer terror. The bully knew the game was up. Even his own friends were shouting insults.

"Papa, I'm sorry," he told his father. "Dr Sameer stopped me from taking the test because I hadn't studied for it and so, I cheated. I just made it all up that he was very unfair to me and picked on me. That's why I told you to complain to Mr Boyle."

Mr Chaudhury looked as if he'd swallowed a huge fish. "But-but-but—"

"Papa," went on Adam Butt. "Mr Boyle is the one who made us sign that petition." Then, turning to Mr Boyle, he said, "You were the one, Mr Boyle, who said Dr Sameer was a very bad teacher although we know he was very good. Mr Boyle, remember, you said you'd expel the lot of us if we didn't sign that letter?"

"I-I-I—" Mr Boyle looked as if he'd swallowed a huge frog and couldn't speak. Then he found his voice. "Silence!" he thundered. Everyone became quiet and still. Then, turning to Mr Chaudhury, he said, "You were the one, Mr Chaudhury, who had complained about Dr Sameer. You were the one who told me to get rid of him." He stabbed his finger at Mr Chaudhury every time he said 'you'. There was a stunned silence after this statement.

Mr Chaudhury was not the seventh richest man in the country without reason. He was used to always getting his way. And now, this lowly headmaster was actually confronting him! An ugly look crossed his face.

"Mr Boyle. It is true. I complained about the teacher. And part of this was because my son had not told me the entire truth." He shot his son a dark look. "But I never told you to fire him. I never told you to make the children sign a false petition. I never told you to make my son tell all kinds of lies.

"The old headmaster, Mr Dimpleby, would have explained things to me. He would have called the teacher to his office, and made us both talk. But you! You have some kind of grudge against Dr Sameer. That's why you used my complaint to get your own back on him."

Mr Boyle stood with his mouth wide open. But Mr Chaudhury hadn't finished.

"And you are a cheat, Mr Boyle. You told me that if your school placed an order for my toilet paper, you would expect to be paid a commission." Mr Boyle opened his mouth to say something, but Mr Chaudhury held up his hand. "Mr Boyle, I did not force you to buy my toilet paper. You offered to buy it yourself. So, don't give me any more lies that I tried to bribe you."

There was a roar from the room. The boys were thumping Dickie on his back, calling him a jolly good fellow for speaking out. Pandemonium broke out. Some of the students jumped up on to the stage and began tossing the toilet rolls to the students below, who tossed them back, as if it were a game of throw-ball.

More and more rolls kept falling down from the fly loft, and most surprisingly, seemed to be aimed only at Mr Boyle. It was as if someone was sitting up in the fly loft, aiming at Mr Boyle, and also at Mr Chaudhury, although the maximum were reserved for the headmaster. Butt Extra-Soft Luxury Toilet Rolls began flying around, a fun free-for-all.

Zara, who was still seated between her parents, was staring at the whole scene unfolding before her. Then, Mr Boyle ran out of the hall, his short legs beating a hasty retreat, pelted all the while with toilet rolls.

"Get out, Bully Boyle. We want Dr Sameer again."

The students all took up the chorus. They went up to Dr Sameer and lifted him up on their shoulders, cheering for him. They also lifted up Zara, cheering for her too. Her glasses fell off as she was carried horizontally on their shoulders and disappeared among the feet of the students.

"Hip-hip-hurray for Zara and Dr Sameer. Three cheers for them!" In deference to Dr Sameer's age and position, he was set down, but Zara was carried about. "Three cheers for Zara who won the Science Talent Cup for our school. We never cheered for you then, Zara. So, we're making up for it now."

Zara, while being carried, looked up at the fly loft above the stage. She saw a big, burly figure looking down at her. She smiled at it, and it smiled back, its dark eyes twinkling. Then, Adam Butt and his father came up to Dr Sameer.

"I am truly sorry," said Mr Chaudhury, "for how you were treated. I know you are a fine teacher. I will surely punish this boy for telling lies about you." He gave Adam Butt a hard look. "My son is going to apologise to you in front of the whole school."

Adam Butt looked at Dr Sameer sheepishly.

They were up on the stage and all the students were quiet once more. "Sir, I'm really sorry," he said. "I'm sorry I told lies about you. We all know you are the best teacher in the school. I promise you, I'll work hard like you told me to do. But please, please don't leave our school."

The students clapped after this speech. Mr Matthew, one of the senior-most teachers, went up on to the stage and told the students to return to their classes. There was a general commotion as they went back, excitedly discussing the events of the day. It was only after the whole auditorium was empty that both videographers stopped their recording.

The hall emptied, and only Zara, her parents and her friends were left. The videographers began gathering their cameras and big tripods. They came up to the group.

"We've got to give this both to the board of governors and to the press," said one of them.

"Hahaha," laughed the other. "Let's send

it to them right now. Serves that Boyle right. Thought no end of himself! Dr Sameer, you are a star."

Dad still looked dazed. Mom too.

"Ha-ha! Our plan worked," said Zara to her friends.

And it was only then that Mom noticed. She let out a shriek.

◆◆◆

Chapter 33

All's Well That Ends Well

Mom shrieked so loudly that Dr Sameer thought his wife was having a heart attack.

"Seema, it's fine. Everything's worked out well," he said, grabbing her by the shoulders, afraid she'd fall.

Mrs Sameer pointed with a shaking finger at Zara. "Where are your — ?" She couldn't complete her sentence. The words seemed to be stuck in her throat. Dr Sameer looked at his daughter.

"My goodness, Zara. Where are your glasses?"

Her friends too chimed in. "Zara, did you drop them when we carried you around? Should we help look for them?"

Zara blinked slowly. How was she to tell them about Joom? No, no, she couldn't. They'd think she'd gone bonkers, stark staring mad.

"My glasses?" she said. "I don't need glasses any more. I can see as well as any of you. If not better."

Ramu was the first to test her. "Read this," he said, thrusting a paper from a medicine bottle into her hands. (Please don't ask how or why Ramu was carrying the literature from a cough mixture bottle. And we all know that the print on those papers is so small, you sometimes need a microscope to read it.)

"Sure," said Zara. "Dextromethorphan Polistirex. Extended release suspension. Cough suppressant."

She was about to continue reading the fine

print when Dad stopped her. "Why didn't you tell us this before? Since when did you start seeing clearly?"

"Mom, Dad, I told you this morning," said Zara. "But you didn't pay any attention to me."

"But you came to school with glasses," said Mimi. "Why did you wear them if you don't need them?"

Zara swallowed. She hated telling lies, but how would they ever believe her adventure with Joom? "They were fake glasses," she said. "The ones you wear when you're six years old and play doctor-doctor. I had a pair lying with me."

Mom, who'd remained silent all this time, now suddenly found her voice. "When did you find out you can see clearly?" she demanded.

"Mom, I don't really know. Since yesterday. My eyes felt all watery and I rubbed them and washed my face, and then saw I could see."

"Hey *rabba*," said Mom. "God has shown mercy on us."

"But we have to go to Dr Ravi for a complete check-up," said Dad, always the practical one.

By this time, they had left the hall. They passed Mr Boyle's office, but there was a big lock on the door. The headmaster was nowhere to be found, and his car was missing from his parking slot.

"Phew! What a day!" Dr Sameer said, wiping his sweaty forehead. There were students walking around freely, with teachers ordering them to get into their classes. They exchanged high-fives with Zara and wished Dr Sameer deferentially, like they used to before. "Dr Sameer, we want you as our headmaster," many said. Dad didn't respond. He looked dazed, as if he couldn't believe what had happened.

Mimi and Pixie were especially delighted for Zara.

"We're so happy for you," said Pixie. "Now, you needn't leave our school. I don't think Bully Boyle will be coming back any time soon."

Zara hugged them both and thumped Dickie and Ramu on their back.

"I don't know how to thank you all," she said. "It was an outrageous plan, but it worked. Thank you for taking up those toilet rolls. It must have been so tiring, climbing up three flights of stairs."

"Did you naughty children plan this?" Mom asked, her eyes twinkling.

"Mom, it was just a shot in the dark," said Zara, "and Ramu was the real mastermind."

"Miss, honestly, we thought it would be a harmless joke dropping toilet rolls on Mr Boyle," said Ramu. "And Dickie really helped us. He knew exactly where the rolls were stored."

"It was a bit of a problem telling our parents we had to come after school hours, but we managed," said Pixie with a big grin. "Mimi and

I both said we had to finish our science project and could work on it only in school."

"I said the same to my parents," said Ramu, showing a flash of even, white teeth.

"Pixie did the most climbing into the fly loft to store the rolls. She's really fast," said Mimi, giving her friend a squeeze. "We told Dickie to sit there in the loft and stack the rolls, however many we could get up. I think there were over a thousand. Not easy to stack."

"I had to only move the scenery and other stage props to one side," said Dickie modestly. "Not much I did."

"Of course you did a lot," said Ramu, and the others chimed in in agreement.

"Dickie, you found your voice at last," said Zara. "It was you who told Mr Boyle that he'd forced you all to sign the petition. And you said that in front of the whole school. You're a hero for speaking the truth."

"You gave me the courage, Zara," said Dickie.

All this while, Dad was quiet, listening to the conversation, not saying a word.

"Didn't the janitor see you?" Mom asked. "How could you children transport all those rolls up three flights of stairs without being seen?"

"I guess we just got lucky. He didn't come this side at all," said Mimi.

"There's only one thing that puzzles me," said Ramu. "Zara, I thought you'd be the one tossing the rolls down, but you were sitting there in the auditorium. Who was it up in the fly loft, aiming those rolls so perfectly?"

"Oh, I have a secret friend," said Zara, laughing. "A genie friend."

"Aww, c'mon!" the children said. "Tell us who it is."

But before they could answer, Dad, who had remained silent all this while, spoke, "I am very proud of all of you. Zara, you especially have taught me that we all have a voice, and we should not put up with injustice. Now, I think it high time that you all go and attend your classes."

"Yes, Dr Sameer, sir," they all said obediently.

"I better go too," said Zara, a cheeky grin on her face.

Just then, a tall, important-looking man in an elegant grey suit came up to them.

"Are you Dr Sameer?" he asked, proffering his hand to Dad. "I am Anthony Ratnam, head of the board of governors. Let's go to my office. I have some good news for you."

Dad left with the gentleman. Zara turned and saw Joom next to her.

"Don't worry, little one," he said. "I've used an invisible spell. Only you can see me. And see, what I told you was true. Miracles happen if you believe in them."

Epilogue

The events of Summerdale High School were splashed across all the papers. The board of governors were furious that the school's fair name had been dragged through the mud. Without any further ado, Mr Boyle was dismissed, and Dr Sameer took his place. He made a solemn promise to Zara and Mom that he would no longer be a wimp. "Or else another Boyle will stomp all over you," said Mom.

Because of all the mental anguish he had undergone these last few months, he was compensated with a big cash award and tickets for all three of them to visit Disneyworld in California. "This is the least we can do, Dr Sameer," said Mr Anthony Ratnam. "You have always been a pillar of strength for our school."

Zara was so excited when she heard this news. But her parents were happy for another reason, because Los Angeles was in California, and they could still show Zara to the specialist. "But, Mom, I don't need to see any specialist," said Zara. "I can see better than ever."

It was hard for Zara to explain to her parents how she could suddenly see with twenty-twenty vision. They couldn't believe it themselves, and in fact, even Dr Ravi was astounded when he checked her eyes. She told them the 'official' version, that one fine day she woke up and could see perfectly.

Of course, she couldn't tell them about her adventure with Joom, or even of her friendship with him. She felt bad for not telling her old best friends, Pixie and Mimi, as well as the new best friends, Ramu and Dickie. But that would be their own little secret, Joom's and hers.

Zara no longer had to leave Summerdale High School. And, since he was now headmaster, Dr Sameer moved to a big house with a garden in Gurugram on the outskirts of Delhi. The school also gave him a brand new car, a big SUV so he could travel quickly and safely to school.

Zara had insisted there be a tamarind tree in the garden, and they'd found the perfect house with tamarind, mango and guava trees growing in the backyard. Joom and Zara continued meeting every night. Zara brought him big glasses of lemonade in the hot summer months and cocoa in the cold winter. And after she returned from her holiday to California, she brought him a big hunk of—yes, you guessed right—Gorgonzola cheese, along with a basket of apples and pears.

"What's this?" Joom asked, poking the cheese. "A bit smelly, isn't it?"

Zara laughed. "It's Gorgonzola cheese, Joom. I tasted it in an Italian restaurant in Los Angeles, and insisted we bring back some. Mom and Dad don't much care for it, so I've brought the entire portion for you. It's smelly, but tastes great with fruit."

"Is that so?" Joom said, a big grin on his face. "Gorgonzola, let me take a bite of you."

They both ate the late-night feast, thinking of all that they'd gone through and how much they'd learnt and grown as individuals. After Joom had had his fill, he let out a big burp.

"Little Zara, that was the best feast of my life," he said. Zara nodded.

Now, if you happen to go to Gurugram in Delhi and come across a house with a tamarind tree, look again carefully. You just might see a genie and a little girl feasting away on its branches.

◆◆◆